THE FIRST-TIME FATHER BABY'S FIRST YEAR

THE ULTIMATE FIRST TIME DADS' GUIDE FROM BABY TO TODDLER

ALFIE THOMAS

For Mirabelle and Ella

BOOK DESCRIPTION

This heartfelt, funny, and insightful book about fatherhood is about a father preparing himself for his newborn baby. This book delves into the nitty-gritty of what it is to be a father while understanding and going through all the changes and challenges.

Penned in a conversational manner, this book will take you on the author's journey of learning about parenting through his experiences. It has great advice for new dads, how to be the best dad to your child, a supportive partner, and look after your own needs as well, all written down with a sprinkling of real-life stories and anecdotes to keep you entertained.

Practical guide for new dads, from your baby's birth to their first birthday.

Newborns don't come with a manual, but *We're Parents!* is the next best thing. Adrian Kulp (a four-time dad himself) offers fast, fun, and easy-to-digest advice that makes it simple for you to step up and do your part as a brand-new dad.

Wondering how to burp your newborn? Not sure how to get them to try solids? Desperate to get them to sleep? This comprehensive guide breaks your baby's first year down into quarterly chunks, offering stage-specific advice, quick reference guides, tutorials, monthly stats and goals, and a healthy dose of humor to help you be a supportive partner and great dad to your little one.

This standout among new dad books includes:

• **Step-by-step how-to**—Find detailed guidance for common situations you'll encounter as a new dad, from soothing and swaddling your newborn to spotting food allergies and baby-proofing your home.

• **Cheat sheet checklists**—Get quarterly checklists of ways you can help around the house, with mom and the baby, and with events and medical appointments.

• **Developmental milestones**—Track your baby's development at a glance with charts that lay out the most important milestones in one place.

Discover how to be the best father and husband you can be with the expert advice inside *We're Parents!*

CONTENTS

INTRODUCTION

Parenting through the perspective of a father / What does a father think about parenting? / I'm a dad. Now what? / Does every dad feel the same way?

A couple of my best friends and I were at a downtown sports bar on a Saturday night watching the LA Lakers and Chicago Bulls basketball game. It was a close game, so all of us were on the edge of our seats, rooting for the Lakers because we lived in Los Angeles (LA). While sipping on our chilled beer and watching the game in anticipation, one of my friends kept receiving repeated calls, and we told him to either accept the call or put his phone on silent mode. He disappeared in between the game, and by the time he returned, the Lakers had won, and the entire bar had erupted into celebrations.

"That was my wife. I have to rush because my son is not feeling well, sorry guys." That is all he said, and he sped out of the bar without us getting the chance to get a word in. While I felt concerned for him, I was also grateful for not having child and family issues in my life. I was 28 years old, single, had a great-paying job in an accounting firm, and marriage and children were nowhere on the horizon for me. My other friend and I joked about how glad we were to not be in his situation, cheered for being single, and drank late into the night, only to wake up with a terrible hangover the following day.

I distinctly remember the next morning. I dragged myself out of bed, made myself a cup of warm brewed coffee, called and asked about his son (who was fine by then; it was about teething issues), and told him how he missed out on a great night. His answer, which made no sense at all was, "Buddy, I'm sure you two had a great time, but I had to be there for my family, and honestly, that was good enough for me." I could not relate to him, and while I said yes, I understood him, I secretly thanked God for not putting me in such a situation.

Fast forward five years, and I can now completely relate to that conversation. Life is funny. I am a father to a three-year-old daughter, and I cannot imagine my life without her. Fatherhood is beautiful and comes with a bag of mixed emotions. I remember when my wife, Anna, told me she was pregnant. I

was ecstatic and began to tear up. I wanted to be the best father to our child, so I decided to prepare myself as much as I could before the delivery of our child. However, when I set out to buy books and attend classes on parenting, I was disappointed that there was not much material available for fathers-to-be. When I asked other friends who were fathers how they prepared for their child, the usual response was 'we winged it, bro,' or 'take it as it comes.' Honestly, that was not helpful at all; I felt so slightly lost and discouraged and decided to read up on a lot of pregnancy books for mothers, which helped me be a better and more understanding husband to my wife, though it did not help me much in what was in store for me as a new father.

Maybe historical and patriarchal stereotypes were at play here; however, I did as much research as I could and began my journey of fatherhood. Hence, here I am today with all my experience to help new fathers cope and navigate the new experience of becoming a parent. It is a rollercoaster of emotions, filled with joy, love, happiness, being overwhelmed, overworked, under-slept, smiles and laughter. Fatherhood changes one's life entirely, and you start feeling differently towards various relationships and aspects of your life. Billions of people have become parents; however, until you become one yourself, you cannot comprehend how incredible the experience is.

It is a given that a child shares a beautiful bond with the mother. Since the child emerges from the mother's womb, it is a symbiotic relationship. However, I feel the connection and bond between the father and the newborn baby are usually overlooked or ignored, which is unfortunate because the father is a parent as well and needs to be involved in the child's life as much as possible.

Throughout the book, I will chronicle the beginning of fatherhood, along with how I prepared, how I helped my wife, the challenges I faced while balancing work and home life, dealing with my child's health, and learning to take care of myself. Becoming a parent is a massive responsibility – emotional, physical, and financial hence think of starting a family when you think you are ready and not 'just because it is the natural next step.' Once you do become a father, remember to be patient with yourself because you are doing the best you can with whatever resources you have available to you.

1

WELCOMING OUR CHILD INTO THIS WORLD

Anna and I met at a common friend's dinner, and we hit it off immediately. We began dating a week after we met and got married a year later. She is a wonderful and supportive partner and an amazing mother. I would also like to add that I am an amazing father. Anna and I had returned from her 5-year-old nephew's Spiderman-themed birthday party and were talking about how adorable the children were. We were sitting on an island in the kitchen, sipping on wine, and she asked me how I felt about starting a family. Of course, we had discussed having a child a few times, but we had never really thought about it in detail. But at that moment, it felt as if I was ready to become a father and start a family with Anna. In retrospect, it could have been the wine and images of cute children at play. This conversation was two years into our marriage. We had a conversation about it the next morning as well and spoke in length about our savings and how we would manage our work-life along with our baby. If Anna and I were to have this discussion three years ago, I would have said no to trying for a baby, but it felt right in the moment because I knew I was as ready as I could be. I knew I was ready to take on the responsibility willingly and give out care and love. You can never be 100% ready, but you will know when you are as ready as you can be. And hence began my journey into perspective fatherhood.

There are numerous couples who have unplanned pregnancies as well. If you are one of them and find yourself in a situation that you had not planned for, it is understandable to be overwhelmed or anxious. However, it is best to take it one day at a time, come to terms with reality, which is you will be a father within the year and have a conversation with your partner about the following issues;

- Accepting the current reality and the situation
- Establishing a financial plan
- Planning and being proactive,
- Reading and researching about everything pregnancy-related
- Preparing for the baby – paternity leave, baby-proofing the house, designing a space for the baby, packing hospital bags, and figuring out a pregnancy plan.

You and your partner are in the same boat; hence both of you need to support each other during this time and make the best of what you have; hurry. If you need support from your friends and family, make sure to reach out to them.

Eleven months into our conversation, Anna was pregnant with our baby girl. She had a rounded belly and was ready to give birth at any given time. It was a Monday, and I was at the office when I received a call from her. "My water has broken; hurry home, please." She had gone into active labor. I left work as soon as possible, rushed home, grabbed our hospital bags that we had prepared in advance, and drove to the hospital.

In Anna's bag, we had packed.

- Nursing bras
- Comfortable pajamas
- Medicines
- Toiletries
- A dressing gown
- Comfortable slippers
- Maternity underwear
- A pack of muslins (to clean up the newborn's bodily fluids)

- Towels
- Maternity pads
- Phone charger
- Going home outfit

For the baby, we packed;

- Baby clothes (sleepsuits and a pack of vests)
- Blanket
- Socks
- Nappies
- Baby wipes
- Car seat

I packed for myself;

- Clothes
- Phone charger
- Toiletries
- Hospital paperwork, ID, and insurance card
- Snacks

It is convenient and time-efficient to have these bags ready in advance a week before your wife's delivery time. This way, you will be prepared whenever your wife goes into labor. All you have to do is load the bags into the car and head to the hospital.

She is coming!

I remember Anna being relatively calm on our way to the hospital. I had called our gynecologist when Anna told me that she was going into labor for them to be prepared when we got there. She was admitted to the room; her vitals were checked and monitored, and then the process began when the doctor told us that Anna was 9 cm dilated. We had prepared a birth plan as well. It is another important tip I would like for everyone to follow. It makes the process of childbirth smoother and irons out any creases or bumps. Anna and I included the following in our birth plan;

- Which hospital or birthing center she would give birth at
- The environment she would like
- Who she wanted in the room
- If she wanted any pain-controlling medications
- Who would cut the umbilical cord

These are common questions, and it is great to have answers to them beforehand rather than scurrying around at the last minute and adding more than what is required on your plate.

While following a birthing plan is wonderful, remember to stay flexible in case of an emergency.

We had decided I would be with Anna in the delivery room. Anna's family and my family were extremely understanding about our decision. Usually, hospitals have policies about how many people are allowed into a delivery room; hence, it is advisable to check beforehand with the hospital and let your family know accordingly. Moreover, ask your partner what she prefers and is comfortable with.

The process was long and tiring for Anna as it was for me. But being there for her, cheering her on, and staying strong really helped her through the entire process. Honestly, it is not an easy process, and hats off to women for going through this. When our baby girl, Ella, came into this world, Anna and I both cried because we were so overwhelmed with joy and exhaustion at the same time. It was a beautiful yet tiring experience. Anna was drained, but when she saw Ella, it was as if she had been reenergized. I knew we would have different experiences of first holding her. I also felt slightly insecure and thought if I'd be able to be as important as Anna in Ella's life, and I checked myself and reminded myself that our process and our love would be different yet present from both ends. Anna held Ella first, and I took a few pictures of their first moments together, and then the nurse handed Ella over to me. I do not think I have been left speechless before, but when I first held my daughter, I was left speechless. She was bundled up in a light pink blanket, her cherubic face matching the color of her blanket. Her eyes were semi-shut, and I like to believe she was smiling at me, but that could also be my delusional happiness speaking. It was like magic, and it was as if I had known her all my life. I held her ever so softly as if she was a fragile doll. I had anticipated this moment for a while, I had read up and researched as much as I could, but when the experience was felt in reality, no amount of reading or hearsay could cover how I felt in the moment. I was overwhelmed by a feeling of love and the need to keep her safe. 'She is here and safe with me, Anna. I am a father now,' I remember telling Anna. The moment was incredible for both of us.

Fathers play a vital role during labor and delivery; hence it is essential for you to, as a father and a partner, give it your best. With practice and education, you can become an excellent partner, so do not be harsh on yourself. Following are a few tips you can follow once your partner goes into labor. All individuals are unique, so all the tips may or may not apply to you, but you will know what your partner wants to be attuned to her needs and be her anchor.

1.   Be a role model to your partner in labor. To put it mildly, it is difficult going through labor. Hence strange things begin to happen to a woman's body. During this moment, observe your partner's breathing pattern. Notice if she is breathing in a shallow manner or if her breathing is fast-paced. Instead of telling your partner, act out an effective method of breathing for her pain management, which will help her cope with the pain and stay relaxed. An effective breathing method is taking a deep breath in and a deep breath out repeatedly. Hence, model it visually for her since it will be much easier for her to do the correct breathing when she sees you doing it. The same goes for body language. If you see your partner hunched up or sitting tensed up, instead of saying 'straighten up' or 'sit straight,' you can emulate her posture and shake it out, and she will visually be able to see the effect. In essence, think of yourself and remember that non-verbal communication is assertive. During labor, too much conversation can annoy your partner; it is a physically and mentally demanding situation, after all; hence it is easier to be led with ideas rather than thinking about what she should be doing herself. Plus, it is a thoughtful way of being

there for your partner and giving them support when they
need it the most.

There are different methods of breathing you can practice
during labor. Focused breathing is one. When this technique
is practiced, it helps to interrupt the transference of pain
signals to the brain and stimulate the release of endorphins
which work as pain relief hormones n the body. Another
technique of breathing is abdominal breathing, which is often
referred to as diaphragmatic breathing. This technique works
in tandem with the abdominal muscles. While inhaling, the
abdomen moves outwards, and when exhaling, it moves
inwards. If you do yoga or practice meditation, you will be
familiar with abdominal breathing. The benefit of this
technique of breathwork is that it changes brain waves by
decreasing stress hormones, reducing blood pressure, and
increasing oxygen levels. Work on the breathing technique
that works positively for your partner. In order to become
familiar with these breathing exercises, you can practice them

beforehand, alone or with your partner, because practice makes perfect!

2.   Be her number one cheerleader. It is extremely valuable to the process of labor and delivery. It can be hard to remember positive things to say in the labor room, and it is easier to say negative things such as 'you look tired' or 'this is taking long.' Positive reaffirmation is important because it will make your partner feel better. The hack is that you should think of yourself as an actual cheerleader as if you are on the sidelines of a marathon and your partner is running by. Imagine yourself in that situation. I am sure you would definitely not say 'you are tired' or 'is this hard?' while she was running by. Instead, try working with positive affirmations such as 'what you've created is,' 'you're nearly there,' and 'the finish line is coming up.' If your partner has been administered pain medication and doesn't look as active prior to the epidural, believe me, she is. Even during a cesarean, she looks passive; she may not be, so bring your A-game to the labor room.

3.   Be the DJ. Music is powerful in labor. It can change the tone and mood, give you energy, and keep you calm. Moreover, it can be fun too. Suggest making a playlist together. The playlists can be calming, relaxing, active, or even favorites. You can make a playlist of songs that make your partner happy. Get some good equipment, such as a Bluetooth speaker, or play it on your phone. Music acts as a coping mechanism for relaxation. When you get to the hospital and get situated, go ahead and get the playlist on. Sometimes, we forget in the entire chaos, but remember to do this. Scientifically, music has the ability to deepen and slow down breathing (which is helpful, as mentioned previously), reduces stress, and enables adequate physiological functioning.

4.   Hydration. Be the water boy throughout the labor period because hydration is key for contractions and labor. Dehydration can lead to strange labor patterns or can stop labor altogether. Plus, keeping hydrated is extremely doable. However, I suggest you do it strategically – have a bottle with a straw because it is easier to manage in whatever position your partner may be in. You can even vary the type of liquids, such as electrolytes water, Gatorade, and coconut water. Instead of asking your partner if she is thirsty or wants a sip, just take a bottle with a straw and put it next to her mouth. Imagine yourself as a trainer in the NBA, standing on the sidelines. You see trainers come out with squirt bottles and just hold them up so they can squirt water into the player's mouth. That is your goal as well. You will want to see her taking a couple of sips between every few contraptions. Remember to hydrate yourself as well, please, because you are the caregiver. You can only do your best if you take care of yourself as well. Staying hydrated can become more vital if the mother opts for an epidural. Hence, staying hydrated and loading up on fluids before getting the anesthesia will decrease the chance of low blood pressure and will also help in recovery post-delivery.

5. **Have, give and eat snacks because snacking is vital.** Make a snacks shopping list beforehand. You should be eating during labor, and so should your partner. I do not mean a three-course meal, but rather intermittent and healthy snacking. It helps labor progress and fuels you along the entire process. The hospital you and your partner choose to give birth at may have a policy that restricts eating during a certain point in labor, with epidural, or at a certain time of labor, so please do check in with your hospital before. Do not ask your partner if she is hungry. Instead, unwrap something and hand it to her. Giving something to eat rather is much more effective than thinking about what to eat. The snack and water tips are equally important when you get the baby home as well because hydration and eating while breastfeeding is good for the mother. If she sits down to feed the baby, you put a bottle with a straw and some snacks for her as well.

6. **Comforting touch.** It is important to re-center your partner during the process. You can do a light massaging touch and massage the head slightly; this will assure her you are there by her side and she is safe. A gentle and comforting touch floods our nerve gates with pleasure sensations; hence the mother will not be focusing on uncomfortable sensations. You can also apply counterpressure at this time if that works

better for your partner. This practice will help ease your partner's mind and bring her back to a relatively calmer space. She may not like you doing it, but ask her to communicate that to you, so you know what to do instead. Remember not to take anything personally. If your partner is in transition, touching or rubbing may become slightly annoying, so be wary and know what your partner wants at the moment.

7.   **Ignorance is bliss.** During pushing and birth, do not let the mother know she has pooped (it is a completely natural process during pregnancy, and it also signals the finish line). Instead, sprinkle some peppermint essential oil onto the mat under your partner. Be by her side, hold her hand, and keep peeking to see the baby's head. Help her tune into her body and listen to when it is time to push and how long to push for.

Nobody knows her body better than herself, so help her tune into her body. If she is on an epidural, she may need help regarding when and how long to push for. Maybe you can choose to be silent while the nurse or doctor does that. Either you are coaching your partner during the final push, or the medical team does that.

Labour is a demanding situation, more so for the mother. Hence, you and your partner may be at your wit's end. However, try to do your best for your partner and know that you are doing the best you can!

Bringing our angel home

Luckily, Anna had a smooth delivery without any hiccups, and Ella was in fine health. Hence, the doctors gave us the go-ahead to head home after a night in the hospital. Your hospital will arrange all the items you'll require for your child once you get discharged and head home with your baby. Make sure you grab any extra diapers, a bulb syringe, an infant hairbrush, and wipes on your way out. Extra items go a long way. Moreover, your hospital may also provide you with numerous lotions, soaps, formula samples, and creams for your baby and the mother. Another checklist to have prepared before getting discharged from the hospital is your baby's health screening checklist. Getting professional medical advice from doctors comes in handy; thus, take your time and ask the medical team if you or your partner have any concerns. Moreover, the nursing team at the hospital will check the temperature and jaundice levels, oversee any vaccines, and schedule a hearing screening.

We headed home happily, going from a family of two to three overnight. Anna, Ella, and I, a picture-perfect family. It is essential to have a car seat prepared for the baby and know how to strap in your newborn with all the harnesses and latches. Anna and I had pre-planned this, so we had the house baby-proof and ready for Ella. For Ella, we had chosen a lilac theme for her nursery. Set against a floral wallpaper lay Ella's white DaVinci Kalani crib. For Anna, I had purchased a comfortable cream-colored armchair with a footstool. I had no clue how much time Anna and I would be spending on that chair, and it became our second bed.

The novelty of our situation had us slightly overwhelmed. I believe I was more anxious and nervous than Anna, and I tried not to be overt about it. Even though my mind was an encyclopedia on everything baby-related, living in the moment, I was pretty uncertain about what to do next. A quote by John Green really resonated with me in this situation. "The nature of impending fatherhood is that you are doing something that you're unqualified to do, and then you become qualified while doing it." Anna sensed that and told me to take a deep breath and said the following simple words to me, 'let's go with the flow. We've got this.' At that moment, those were the most reassuring words. If you find yourself in a situation similar to mine, repeat that phrase to yourself because, honestly, you have got this, and just go with the flow.

Now that we have covered the incredible moments of feeling fatherhood and an immense amount of unconditional love, let's get down to reality. You will most probably be dealing with the following issues once you and your partner return home;

Baby's sleep pattern – Are they sleeping enough?

The aim is to make sure your baby sleeps throughout the night. It sets a pattern and allows the baby to develop the habit of sleeping through the night. However, do not be surprised if your baby sleeps a lot during the day in the first few days, though this cycle will get regulated eventually. Meanwhile, the mother's and the father's sleep patterns will be in sync with the baby's sleep pattern; hence, it is an adjustment period for the entire family. The good news is that everyone does adjust. Moreover, make the most of the period when your baby is awake and establish a bedtime routine, irrespective of how young your child may be. It is a great pattern to develop early on. When you do put your child to bed, please place them on their back; it is the best position for a newborn baby.

Did the baby just hiccup or let out a gasp? (Discerning between the two can be difficult initially)

Changing the baby's clothes – How do I do it without hurting the baby? Nervous while handling your baby?

We've all been there. After all, newborn babies are so fragile. Therefore, make sure you handle them with gentle and soft care, and in order to develop their head and neck muscles, you should use your hand as a support. In order to change the baby's clothes as gently as possible, support their head while maneuvering their clothes around their small body. Rather than slipping the shirt or pants as is, gather the sleeves or the seams, as it is easier to dress your baby that way. Moreover, keep in mind that you must hold your baby upright and support their neck and head when zipping or buttoning them into clothes.

Feeding times and how to decipher what the baby wants

If your partner pumps her breast milk and you are on night feeding duty, make sure late-night feeding is just that, do not try to play with the baby at this time since it might disrupt their pattern. Remember to burp the baby after every two ounces. To all the fathers out there reading this, a mother breastfeeds her newborn for the first few weeks. However, she may choose to pump her breast milk once the nursing period is established. This is where you step in and can divide the feeding time between yourself and your partner. Not only does it relieve your partner and gives her time to tend to her personal time, but it also helps to create a bond between you and your child – what more could you want? Moreover, a newborn will usually cry out for milk, to be held, to be fed, or for a diaper change. Hence, if the baby is crying or squirming, know that it is your cue to check the aforementioned needs.

Not so angelic anymore

While it was absolutely wonderful spending time with Ella and dividing tasks with Anna, everyone was running high on emotions and low on sleep. Anna and I had spoken in detail and in-depth about our particular roles and duties, which proved to be helpful; however, sometimes, those duties may be overlooked in all the chaos of settling down and establishing a routine, which is okay. I believe the manta 'it is okay. I/we can do this really helped Anna and I initially during the postpartum period. Furthermore, Anna and I would make sure we would alternate our nap, eating, and showering times in order for each of us to function in a healthy manner. I had spoken to numerous friends and family members who told me alarming stories of how they did not shower for three days because they did not find the time or how they forgot to eat for the entire day and ended up fighting with their partner over the smallest of issues – being hangry is real. For the first 96 hours, it was all about diaper changes, breastfeeding, sleeping, and tending to Ella crying out. I felt I was living in a time loop. I would find myself nodding off while holding Ella in my arms.

It had been two weeks since we had returned from the hospital with Ella. She had been fed and was sleeping. Anna and I decided to open a bottle of wine and just have a conversation. I remember taking a few sips, Anna was talking about something she had read in a magazine, and the next thing I knew was that I fell asleep mid-conversation. Anna loves relating this story to everyone. You can imagine the extent of exhaustion. Fortunately, my company had given me two months of paternity leave which really worked out wonderfully for the entire family. I could bond with Ella, support Anna, and help around the house. I was able to focus entirely on what I wanted to do. Of course, children are the most wonderful additional component to a family, but the reality is that it is hard work and effort, especially during the first week when the baby comes home from the hospital. It requires all your dedication – physical, emotional, and financial.

Moreover, you do not just have your partner and baby to tend to, family and friends also want to visit, and honestly, that is the last thing we wanted to do; socialize. It is okay to draw a boundary and tell your friends and relatives that you will be ready to meet when you actually are settled in and ready to meet. However, if your friends and family desperately want to see you and your baby, then they can come to have a peek and could maybe help you out with some chores, such as getting a cooked meal or buying your weekly groceries. I found my best friends to be extremely cooperative and understanding. They would drop in and say hello and drop off a cooked meal. It made our lives so much easier. A couple of times, they came with bottles of wine and dessert, which really helped Anna and I unwind after a long day. Anna and I had decided that we would hire help for the first month to help with household chores, and it turned out to be one of the best decisions we made. I do not know how we would have managed to make the beds or do the laundry with Ella around.

What's more, our house help was so helpful we decided to hire her on a long-term basis. Melissa is still with us and is wonderful with Ella. Caring for a baby is a full-time duty. It would have been extremely difficult for Anna to manage on her own. I am sure she would have managed, but it would have been entirely unfair on her. After all, the baby is ours, not just hers.

2

GETTING PREPARED TO RAISE A CHILD (PRENATAL)

As soon as Anna and I found out she was pregnant with Ella, I went into extreme planning mode after celebrating, of course. We informed our friends and family about our good news, celebrated some more, and then got down to the real business.

Read as much as you can

There is a lot of material available that allows parents to begin planning and sorting out what they need in order to prepare for their newborn baby. As Dwight D. Eisenhower once said, "Plans are worthless, but planning is essential," which very applies to planning for childhood. While Anna began reading books on her reading list, I began reading the books on mine. I was looking to understand how pregnancy works, how I can support my partner, be a good father and caretaker, and how my life would change after our baby arrives. I got hold of a handful of books that provided me with a great understanding and prepared me for what was to come. The types I opted for ranged from how-to to personal experience books. One of my favorites was *The Expectant Father* by Armin Brott and Jennifer Ash. Just make sure you read the latest edition if you do end up buying it. Moreover, there is a wide range of material available online, from personal blogs to official papers.

Honestly speaking, when I first began to read the books on my list, it felt daunting, and I wondered if I would be able to do everything the books advised or retain all the knowledge it was throwing out at me. There were times when I would read a page and put it down in frustration because it made me feel overwhelmed. Sometimes, if I liked a particular book more, I would re-read it and visualize myself doing what I was reading, which made it easier for me to retain all the new information. However, eventually, my anxiety decreased, and I actually started enjoying the content. There was so much I did not know about pregnancy, childbirth, and childrearing, so I felt as if I had unlocked a whole new world. Plus, researching myself proved beneficial in the long run for Anna and me. I was not pestering her constantly to explain things to me, or she did not have to sit me down and explain how things worked. It is a small amount of effort you are putting in for a great return.

Watch videos

What helped me further was watching informative videos and listening to audiobooks as well. If you are not a book person, videos may work for you. They are more interactive and will keep you engaged. While reading is great, I feel watching videos allows me to understand the technical know-how more easily. I tend to understand things better when I can view them visually. Hence, I enjoyed watching videos more. I learned how to assemble a baby cot by watching, how to install the baby car seat, how to change diapers (yes, I did that), how to swaddle a baby, and how to burp a baby all through videos. Additionally, videos are not hard to come by. The Internet has got you covered, so make the most of it. You have no excuse to slack here!

Speak to doctors

Another mode of preparation Anna and I thought to be very helpful was speaking to pediatricians. We have a few friends who are pediatricians, so we got in touch with them to ask them a few general questions about babies' health. If you have any friends or family who happen to be doctors, I advise you to do the same. We discovered there are quite a few health concerns a newborn baby is born with, such as jaundice, skin conditions, feeding, and fever. It is common for newborn babies to develop skin conditions right after they enter this world. Fortunately, most of these skin conditions are short-lived, so there is no need to worry. Jaundice affects most newborn babies. Hence, before getting the mother and the baby discharged, the hospital staff checks the jaundice levels of the baby. While jaundice goes away naturally in some babies, it stays on in some for a longer period, requiring adequate treatment in the hospital. Moreover, the pediatrician told us to look out for any signs of jaundice upon our return home by observing our baby's skin color and signs of dehydration – dehydration normally results in fewer wet diapers. Any serious infection will usually be indicated through mild to high fever in a newborn baby or changes in the baby's behavior. If your baby is a month old, then he/she will have to be taken to the hospital.

One of the major concerns with newborn babies is feeding and regulating their feeding patterns. The pediatrician said newborn babies feed every one-and-half- to three hours in the first few days, and it takes around three to four weeks to establish a set routine. Moreover, an indicator of your baby being fed enough is if six or more diapers are changed in a day and if two yellowish bowel movements are passed. Moreover, after the baby is fed, they will usually spit up, mostly accompanied by a burp. If your baby does vomit consistently after feeding, take them to the hospital. Lastly, do not worry about weight loss in the first 10 to 14 days. They go back to their original birth weight within the first two weeks. These tips proved really helpful to Anna and I, and our minds were put at ease. Usually, new parents go into a frenzy, rightfully so, if their baby is not adhering to what is considered normal or healthy. Thus, knowing the basics of newborn babies' health will allow you to navigate the initial days at home in a calmer and more knowing manner. I also felt slightly more informed because I accompanied Anna to as many doctor's appointments as I possibly could. Routine checks do not just help you be more in sync with the pregnancy but also allow you to raise any concerns or questions you may have. While I do have a demanding job at an accounting firm, I managed to make it to most appointments because Anna created a schedule that allowed me to be there as much as possible.

Attend birthing and parenting classes

The next agenda on my preparation list was birthing classes. These classes are important in preparing, not only for the mother but for the father as well. Truth be told, I was hesitant at first because I had a fear of being the only father at the birthing classes we had signed up for, but I realized I was doing it for myself, my wife, and our baby, and the fear disappeared itself. By the time the classes were wrapping up, I had found myself relieved that I had come across numerous men like myself who shared the same worries and concerns as I did.

I believe parenting solely focuses on motherhood and the mother doing everything, which is unfair, to say the least. The father has an equal role and must take responsibility beyond impregnating. Birthing classes provide parents to be with information on labor, the process of birth, choices about pain relief, how a husband can support his wife or partner through the entire process of giving birth, parenting, and the challenges in the initial months and breastfeeding (which is the mother's area of expertise, but it helps to be informed about the process).

Birthing classes also provide you with the golden opportunities to ask all the questions you have on your mind, get advice, and speak to other parents. For me, my first birthing class was extremely nerve-racking and exciting. I was one of those eager students who wanted to sit in the front row, ask all the questions and soak in all the information that was being given out. While Anna thought it was cute, I am sure the other fathers in the class did not think so. I made some great friends during these birthing classes. Since they were in the same stage as I was, I was able to connect with them more easily, and they seemed more relatable than most of my friends. Do not get me wrong. I love my friends, though they are all in different stages of parenthood; hence, I found it relieving that I could talk to expecting fathers and share our stories and concerns. Knowing that there were so many more fathers-to-be like me felt comforting, as I was not the only one who was excited yet nervous, happy yet anxious.

I believe birthing classes helped Anna and I work better as a team through the entire pregnancy, up until the moment she gave birth. Since I had attended all the classes with her, I knew what to expect and was more confident and supportive during each stage of labor. Moreover, what I learned in the classes gave me the confidence to deal with all the new issues and challenges when we returned home with Ella. Rather than being a deer caught in headlights, I was on my A-game. You do not have to go much further than your local hospital to find out about birthing classes. If you search online, you will also find a list of birthing classes there. Anna and I picked the weekend classes because I could attend them. Decide which classes suit your partner and you best, and then figure out what day works for you two. If you want to be entirely involved, I suggest you opt for the weekend classes, as that way, work does not overlap with the schedule.

While I was finding out about birthing classes at our hospital, I came across antenatal classes just for men, which I did not know existed up until that moment. Did you know? Such classes are run solely by men who are also fathers for men who are becoming fathers. Being the eager beaver that I am, I signed up for these as well. If you are wondering how I managed to attend these and the ones with Anna, I can let you in on the secret. I took them one after the other, which was more convenient for me. While it did get tiring at most times, it was fruitful.

At the men-only classes, I figured out the type of father I wanted to be and what I expected from myself and Anna on this journey. A lot of introspection was required from my end, and I was able to learn more about ways of interacting with our baby and how to be more involved in taking care of the baby and its needs. One of the main differences between the men-only and joint birthing classes was that issues such as the impact of having a baby on a relationship, money matters, sex, and postnatal depression were discussed. These classes were easy-going, and I always had a good laugh during them, made some great friends, and learned valuable lessons. If you do not have the time to do both, it is entirely alright. You can opt to attend one, and if you have a clashing appointment that cannot be missed on the day of the class, you can ask your partner to fill you in on what was taught.

Speaking to new parents and experienced parents

By the time Anna and I decided to try for a baby, many of our friends and family were already parents. This worked out in my favor because I got the chance to ask my friends and family members a lot of questions I had on my mind. Remember my best friend who rushed out of a Lakers game on a Saturday night to tend to his baby? Well, he became my go-to person for all my father-related queries. He took me to a couple of playdates with his group of dad friends, and I noticed how so many fathers seemed natural at what they were doing. Those occasions actually helped me calm the fear I had of not being a good enough father. It is a terrifying thought, and I keep on reiterating this statement only because I want you to know you are not alone in feeling the way you are. Socializing with other dads turned out to be quite helpful.

Being around fathers helped me get a perspective on how different men are as fathers, as well as gave me a real-time chance at viewing how to handle children.

I had had a rough and long day at work because I was juggling between office work and speaking to builders and contractors about the nursery room for Ella. Anna wasn't having the best of days at home either. When I got home, I just wanted to watch some Netflix, have pizza, and spend time with Anna, but Anna's mom and sister were gone. While I was slightly annoyed that I could not enjoy my private time with Anna, I also realized we both could use our own space. So, I decided to meet my group of dad friends, which turned out to be a massive mood lifter for me. If you do find yourself overwhelmed beyond belief or mentally and physically exhausted throughout the journey and do not want to burden your pregnant wife, the group of dad friends is a really great place to unwind and vent your emotions. I found myself doing that, and they offered me an open space to talk about my feelings without being judged. What's more, they gave me reassurance, and I actually felt better after speaking to them. Anna and I have a great understanding between us, but there were moments throughout the journey where I felt Anna had a lot going on herself; therefore, I turned to my 'Dads' friends quite a bit.

Paternity leave time

Since our pregnancy was planned, I had requested the Human Resources (HR) department at my office well in advance about my paternity leave. California is one of the few states that allow and offers a form of paid family leave. Through this program, an employee can get up to six weeks of paid leave and receive 55% of their salary. I had opted to take off 12 weeks and was getting half my salary for six weeks, so it worked out well for me. There is a misconception that paternity leave is a minivacation. Reality check – it certainly is not. I believe it helped me immensely, not only in terms of providing physical and emotional help to Anna but also in bonding with Ella in her first few months. Before I spoke to the HR department, Anna and I sat together and decided on a few important factors which you can take into consideration as well. One of the first things to do while planning paternity leave is;

1. Plan in advance. This works out in your favor as well as your office's favor. Inform your office once you have confirmed when you are planning to utilize your paternity paid leave. Moreover, planning your paternity leave in advance allows you to save up on leaves accordingly.

2. Figure out shifts between yourself and your partner. Most parents take maternity and paternity leave together, and some even alternate their leaves. You and your partner need to

decide what works best for you two – financially, emotionally, and personally.

3. Find out your office policy on paternity leave.

Making our home baby proof

One of the things Anna was most excited about was planning Ella's nursery. I started feeding off Anna's nesting vibes, and both of us went into a deep planning and baby-proof mode. As exciting as it sounds, it is a long and tiresome, as well as costly project to undertake, but one that needs to be, regardless. To begin with, I conducted a safety test for our house. What does that mean, you ask? Well, I wanted to see how safe our house was for our baby. Even though Ella would not be crawling around till around six months, I wanted to be as prepared as I could be rather than leaving things till the last minute. While it was difficult to manage a home improvement and revamp project, it was also fulfilling to know that Ella would have a safe space to move around in.

Moreover, preparing for a child takes effort and time, so the word weekends disappeared from my life. Now, my weekends mostly revolved around birthing classes, doctor's appointments, and home projects. Gone was the 28-year-old drinking beer at a bar on a Saturday night – he was replaced by super dad-to-be (me). It is time-consuming, yes, but it is doable. At times, I felt stretched beyond my means, and there were moments when I wanted to give up, which is okay. We are human, after all, so make sure to give yourself the space to relax as well. Back to the house safety test. To begin with,

1. Conduct a home safety test.

- If you have any arms and ammunition at home, please unload the arms, lock the arms and ammunition separately in a cupboard and store the keys in a place known only to you. Install smoke detectors in the house.
- Store products such as dishwasher pods, medicines, detergent, and soap dishes out of the child's reach.
- Install sturdy baby height structures.
- Install gates on stairways and any exit or entry point.
- Install electrical outlet covers.

- Put edge bumpers on furniture with sharp edges.
- Install a lid lock on your toilet.
- Conceal any wires and cords and make use of cord holders.
- View things from the baby's perspective. Get down on all fours in order to see things you may not see standing up.

2. Prepare your house for overnight visitors.

If you and your partner are expecting any overnight visitors once your baby is born, prepare your home for them. Have the towels, sheets, and toiletries ready for them. Once I returned to work after my paternity leave ended, Anna's mother moved in for a couple of weeks to help Anna with Ella. Being prepared beforehand really saved us from running around last minute with Ella and getting the guest room ready for my mother-in-law.

3. Spring clean the house

- Before starting your cleaning frenzy, make sure you wear gloves, and if your wife is helping you clean, make sure she definitely wears gloves because pregnancy causes the skin to become sensitive. Since cleaning products have chemicals in them, it is best to keep your skin protected.
- Open all the windows in your house (if you live in a

colder area, keep them open if it is not too cold). Keeping windows allow for ventilation and air circulation, which improves the air quality within the house.

• Start cleaning knobs, switches, handles, the kitchen counter, the kitchen sink, basically anything you touch on a regular basis. These areas tend to gather germs because we use them more frequently.

• Dust the home a couple of times before the baby arrives home. Dust allergies are the last thing you want your newborn baby to develop.

• Clean in areas that you would not think of. Hence, any gaps in your sofas, behind the bed and above the shelf. Make sure you dust these areas.

• When we began cleaning, we devised a rule where we would leave our shoes at the front door so as not to get bacteria into the house. We installed a shoe shelf in the entrance area and told our guests to do the same.

4. Reimagine your space with baby belongings

Anna and I love how we did up our house. We handpicked each and everything to make it what it was. However, once we found out Anna was pregnant with Ella, we began to view our space with a baby in mind. We began to make space for our baby in the kitchen as well. How so? I emptied out a couple of drawers where we would place Ella's bottles, Sippy cups, and her baby cutlery and crockery.

Moreover, clean out your fridge and make space for breast milk and formula. I placed a few cloth bags around the house for Ella's toys and any extra clothes we could need. It makes everything neater and more accessible.

5. Designing Ella's nursery

We picked lilac and cream as a color theme for Ella's room. Anna and I spent a lot of time on *Pinterest* creating mood boards and playing around with a lot of textures and palettes until we found the perfect one. It was an exciting project but time-consuming, nonetheless. Yet again, if you are wondering how I managed to take this project on, the secret is utilizing your weekends for these and asking for help from your friends and family. There are some essentials you will need to pick for the nursery;

- Cot
- Bedding
- Changing table
- Dresser
- Storage baskets
- A baby mobile
- Rocking chair or armchair for adults
- Clothes hamper
- A baby monitor
- Nightlight
- Bluetooth speaker

- Baskets for toys
- Shelves for storage
- Ceiling fan

An important tip Anna's sister gave us was to leave space for the room to grow, which turned out to be very handy over the years. The tip is to think long-term – the cot will be replaced by a toddler-sized bed in a few years, more shelves may be added, and so on. Another tip to adhere to (if you are looking to save money and time) is to buy a cot you can turn into a toddler-size bed when the child grows up. There are quite a few options available in stores, and they come with a manual, so it is easy to figure out.

While you are baby-proofing the house, remember to baby-proof the nursery as well. The nursery turned out to be lovely once complete, and it was definitely Pinterest-worthy. While aesthetics matter, remember to keep comfort in mind because you will be spending a lot of time in the nursery as well.

3

T HE IMPORTANCE OF A FATHER IN RAISING A CHILD (0 - 3 MONTHS)

W hen my siblings and I were born, I remember my mother being the primary and sole caregiver. Yes, my father was around on the weekends and on our birthdays; however, my father was not expected to help around the house or help my mother with childrearing. That was a given. Financially supporting the family was the only prerogative. The family system and expectations were quite orthodox. Now that I am a father and can witness parenthood first-hand, I am in awe of my mother. I cannot even begin to think how she managed to raise three siblings by herself. Personally, I would have had a nervous breakdown.

The need to be there for my wife and child does not necessarily emanate from the narrative changing in the 21st century; more so, it stems from my basic need to be there for them and with them because I want to. Fortunately, times have changed, there is more awareness, and the discourse slowly began to evolve in order for the husband to be more involved in childrearing. Being involved in childrearing has multiple benefits; you are more involved in your child's life, which aids the emotional development of your child; you get to develop a deeper bond with your newborn baby, and you are able to support your wife emotionally and physically, and you get the chance to be more proactive in the formative years of your child. It is a win-win situation.

While researching and reading up during Anna's prenatal phase, I came across a quote by Kent Nürburg, which really resonated with me. "It is much easier to become a father than to be one." I couldn't agree more. The real challenges begin when you take on responsibility for bringing a human into this world.

Benefits of early involvement in your baby's life

Your involvement with the process predates when you find out your partner is pregnant and when you start preparing for your child in the prenatal time period. I have been involved since I found out Anna was pregnant, as you must have figured out by now. Due to the fact that I had taken paternity leave for 12 weeks, I was able to be more wholly involved with Ella's first three months. The first three months went by within the blink of an eye, except for the days I was running low on sleep. My best friend – coffee – helped me get through those nights. It has been found that fathers who are more responsive to their baby's cry, fathers who hold, cuddle, and hug them more often and take care of their needs, such as changing diapers and feeding them, have a positive effect on the child's self-confidence and behavior over time. As Sigmund Freud said, "I cannot think of any need in childhood as strong as the need for a father's protection," and I couldn't agree more.

Moreover, studies have proven that children whose fathers are more proactive during their infancy are less likely to show mental health symptoms later on in their childhood. For me, fatherhood is about loving Ella, teaching her and playing with her, setting limits, and being her role model. This unique and powerful role of mine began early on in Anna's prenatal stage. When fathers are involved in the prenatal time, providing the mother with help and support, they are bound to help later on as well, according to research. The relationship is important for healthy development in all domains, including physical, social, emotional, and thinking skills.

From birth, the father's involvement in the baby's caregiving contributes to high levels of secure attachment for the baby, which becomes the vital foundation of a loving bond between both parents and their child over time. Children whose fathers are more involved in daily care, feeding, bathing, and playing with them tend to be more confident and motivated as they grow older. They even enjoy more social connections with their peers, strengthening their social and emotional competency. They also tend to be more patient and later on can handle the stresses and frustrations associated with schooling more easily than children with less involved fathers.

Research also shows these children are also less likely to get into trouble at home, school, or in the neighborhood and experience depression. Those fathers who help, care for, nurture, and play with their babies end up raising children who perform better at school and develop better language and cognitive skills. The time dads devote to children really matters. Research shows that the more time fathers spend on enriching play with their child, such as pretend games and sharing stories, the better that child's math and reading scores are at ages 10 and 11. Involved fathers also support their children's communication skills. Fathers tend to ask more questions than mothers, which builds their vocabulary and conversational skills. The benefits of early involvement also extend to physical benefits. Dads make a difference in the physical area because they tend to play more active tumble games with their children, which builds large muscle groups. This type of play also helps children regulate their emotions and bodies. It is not just the father-child relationship that benefits from your involvement – relations between parents matter too. Husbands and wives who feel satisfied in their relationships tend to be more responsive, affectionate, and confident when caring for their babies and show more self-control when dealing with defiant toddlers. Fathers who are involved in their baby's life – caring for them and playing with them – tend to experience less conflict with mothers, which also strengthens the adult relationship. The everyday moments you are living with your partner and baby help build a strong bond.

Effects of a father's absence from a child's life

While there are multifold benefits to you being involved, I would also like to show you the dark side of not being involved in your child's life. Children who grow up without their father or whose fathers leave are more likely to suffer from behavioral problems, drop out of school, suffer from depression and mental health issues, have financial problems, have problems with anger and aggression, and get into the habit of unhealthy intoxicants. Moreover, if you are an uninvolved father, that has consequences as well.

Your child may be more anxious, emotionally withdrawn, fearful of becoming dependent on others, and more vulnerable. Research demonstrates that children with uninvolved fathers display shortfalls in emotional, social, cognition, and attachment skills. Moreover, they tend to perform below par in all aspects of life. Children emulate what they see their parents do and the type of love and care they receive. Hence, children with uninvolved parents or an uninvolved mother/father will have difficulty developing attachments in their later years, which can also lead to avoiding intimacy in adult relationships.

According to scientific research, fathers undergo neurogenesis during the first few days after the birth of their child and also go through the process of creating and establishing a biochemical bond between themselves and their child. Neurogenesis is a process whereby more neurons are developed by the brain in order to adapt and readapt according to the situations we find ourselves in. Neurogenesis is also connected to learning new things in life; hence, by learning new things, we have the power to grow more neurons. What's more is that this process also affects the newborn baby. The newborn baby is actually expecting the aforementioned bond to be established, to begin with. Miracles of nature!

In the future, children who were solely reared by mothers showed higher occurrences of emotional and psychological issues, more aggression, an increased incidence of addiction problems, and more likely to find themselves in trouble.

Sense of fulfillment

To be honest, it was not these effects and benefits that prompted me to be there for Anna and Ella; it was my personal need and want. Yes, I became more aware of how my presence could benefit Ella, which did play a part in me being more actively involved, but I knew I wanted to be the best father to Ella when I found out Anna was pregnant. It was an innate feeling. There were moments when I would be dejected and exhausted beyond belief, but one smile or giggle from Ella would uplift my mood. When I would hear such anecdotes from new fathers, I would scoff internally and think it to be a fluff story because how can a smile from a baby really change one's mood so drastically? I thought new parents were boring, and their obsession with their newborn was overwhelming – sounds harsh, I know. It took my personal experience to realize it, and I know when the time comes to relate this story to fathers-to-be, they will most likely be scoffing internally at me as well. I became the exact type of father I would make fun of. I think it was God's way of having a good laugh at my cost.

I believe babies have the power to make you happy and deal with stress more effectively. I had had a long and tough day at work. A meeting with a client did not go well, so I returned home in a foul mood, not wanting to interact with anyone and wanting to watch mindless TV and go to sleep. However, when I got home, I was hit with the realization that I was a father now. My stress coping mechanism was very different when I was not a father. Parenting is such a massive task that one automatically puts their emotions in the backseat to look after the needs and wants of your baby. I am not advocating that repression is a good coping mechanism all the time, but it becomes the need of the hour when your baby's needs are more urgent than yours. Thus, when I returned home and saw Anna feeding Ella, I realized I did not have to but wanted to put my bad mood aside and take over from Anna and look after Ella myself. And at that moment, Ella was the perfect antidote to my bad mood. Instead of moping around, I found myself feeding Ella and playing hours of peek-a-boo. Her constant surprise and laughter cheered me up automatically. I made a mental note to thank Ella in the future for being my dose of happiness on days when I needed it the most. When your days are filled with sadness, a baby can give you a sense of purpose and a reason to be happy. Ella and Anna have been my safe haven for so many days that I thought it was just me against the world.

The importance of paternity leave

Taking paternity leave is imperative for the well-being of your family. It is the beginning of developing a relationship between the father and the newborn baby, and you need time to do that. Moreover, paternity leave also reiterates the belief that fathers are not just there to provide financially but also as caretakers and an integral component of the family. For fathers, it is important to be present and active as soon as possible because it allows you to be networked into how the new family runs, works, and interacts right off the bat, and then networking grows and increases over time. It might not work as effectively if the father enters the child's life at 5, 10, or 15 years of age.

The first year after a baby is born is critical for the couple, especially if it is their first child. The best way to strengthen your relationship during this time is to invest your time and effort into fatherhood. Moreover, when new fathers take paternity leave, they are able to take that time to understand what kind of father they will be to their child and what kind of partner they will be after their family grows. Usually, our ideas of fatherhood are developed from seeing our fathers, seeing fathers on TV, or reading about fathers; nonetheless, spending time with your child will help you understand exactly the type of father you can and want to be. It is easier to learn to parent when your partner is around as well.

Research indicates that there is a strong correlation between fathers taking paternity leave and marital stability.

Taking paternity leave allows you to contribute to your child's development. There is evidence that dads usually talk in louder voices as compared to mothers and use more complex language when they communicate with infants, and that turns out to be an important predictor of speech and language development and, eventually, academic readiness. Even the way fathers socialize and play with their children is unique, which promotes important social skills development. Hence, when children eventually grow up and enter a pre-school setting, they are equipped with tools to negotiate with socially complex interactions that happen with their peers. Later on in life, when school starts, the father's emphasis on academic skill-building makes unique contributions to the child's eventual academic achievements and success, which predicts long-term positive outcomes in the child's personal life and is a positive contribution to society as well.

For fathers, their identity as a father will change positively if they are able to take on a more active hands-on role and contribute to caretaking tasks. In terms of benefits for the family unit, paternity leave establishes an upward and positive family trajectory.

Furthermore, paternity leave helps build a new father's confidence. How so? Well, the only way to learn to parent is to throw yourself into it and practice and learn on the job.

This, in turn, will help in developing confidence in making choices and doing tasks centered on your child. Once you do the task at hand and succeed at it, you will be more confident doing it again next time, such as changing diapers, feeding the baby, and burping the baby.

One of the biggest fears of taking paternity leave is hurting your career. I can say this from personal experience. Being in an accounting firm is not easy. It is a competitive environment. I was worried that I would miss out on any promotion opportunities or start lagging at work upon my return. And I am not the only one who had this fear. During my numerous conversations with new and experienced fathers, a lot of them voiced this concern as well. However, during the time I was reading and researching on pregnancy and parenthood, research indicated the opposite of what I feared. Men who take on a more equal part in caregiving and taking paternity leave are actually much happier and satisfied with their jobs. I can vouch for these findings because when I eventually returned to work, I did actually feel happier rather than feeling what I had initially feared. This, in turn, benefits the employer.

There is actual research on the effect parental leaves have on employees. According to the research, three-fourths of employees are most likely to stay with their employer due to the flexibility and allowance of parental leaves they are offered by the organization. These organizations also highlight increased rates of retaining employees as well as more engagement. Moreover, employees return with a happier and more motivated attitude. Therefore, paternity leave should be equally important at organizational levels as well.

Paternity leave also promotes gender equality in the workplace. By allowing paternity leave, the organization is promoting a culture of celebrating women and helping them progress. How so? By essentially enabling the father to be there for his wife and child and act as a support system. It is only fair to give a male employee paternity leave in order to be more active at home with his new family.

Breaking the gender norms

Parenting is synonymous with the mother doing everything possible for the child. Yes, pregnancy is a female-related realm, but that does not mean we shirk away from the other responsibilities that surround it. Besides, mothers are half of the equation of what constitutes a conventional and heterosexual couple in society. Earlier on, society was complacent with the idea that men were redundant when it came to the process of child-rearing and upbringing. However, society dictates a different narrative now, mostly backed by science. Who are we to prove science wrong?

Let us forget science for a few minutes. Is it not just a natural urge to be there for your child and wife? Does the need have to arise from scientific or emotional benefits? Fathers are not merely background props who only provide financially. This harmful stereotype has propagated a generation of absent fathers, and that is not right. I come from a similar family, so I have first-hand experience of how it is to be in a family where the mother is the sole caregiver. Fathers do have an enormous effect on their children. So much so that when fathers are depressed or stressed, their children get as socially, emotionally, and behaviorally affected by it as they would with their mothers. That says a lot about the importance of a father's presence in his child's life. This argument goes beyond gender norms and their impact on children because research suggests that there are no gender differences in the impact of a father's parenting stress on the cognitive development of a child.

Changing the definition of parenthood in society and amongst individuals is imperative. It is assumed that loving and caring for children is a feminine need and urge, and it comes naturally to them. Except it is not entirely true. This idea has harmful implications on the concept of parenthood and what we pass on as the accepted norm from generation to generation. Furthermore, this idea promotes the norm of men taking the back seat because child-rearing is not their forte, and what good can come out of them trying to do a woman's job? It is not a woman's job. Just the way a woman wings it as she goes along the process, so should a man. Nobody is born with the inherent skills of looking after a baby; we learn along the way.

In addition, the idea of fathers in our culture promotes fathers being fun and games and not entirely involved in the child-rearing process. When they do help out, it is considered extremely nice and helpful, as if they are going the extra mile to do what is actually required of them. While I was growing up, I would notice how much appreciation my uncle would receive when he babysat his own children, as if he was doing something extraordinary. Whereas when my aunty would do the same, it would go unnoticed because that was what she was meant to do.

Historically, this idea worked. A world where women were confined to one job – procreating and men were confined to one job – breadwinners. This narrative is obsolete in developed countries, though it still holds a lot of importance in many parts of the world. Yet, as society evolves, so do ideas and concepts. Hence, holding one parent accountable for the child's well-being is wrong.

Moreover, we must consider how our behavior sets a precedent for our children. I know I do not want Ella to internalize these fallacies as she grows up. She needs to see what a healthy functioning family looks like, one that divides the responsibility of parenthood between the mothers and fathers.

4

THE FIRST FEW MONTHS AT HOME WITH ELLA (0 - 6 MONTHS)

Bringing a newborn baby home is a special time for parents. You may be wondering what happens next. Reality kicks in! It is a daunting time for parents, and it is scary as well. Ella relied on us for everything, so there was barely any room for error. However, while it may be challenging, it is also a beautiful time, so remember to soak in all the new memories with your newborn baby because they grow up really fast. A lot of people told us to kiss our freedom goodbye, and while that was true, it is also a temporary period. Get into child-rearing with realistic expectations and understand it will be difficult, and we do a disservice by not talking about the reality of it more openly.

The challenges, memories, and art of reshuffling priorities

Since I had taken a three-month paternity leave from work, I was at home with Anna and Ella. I do not know if you can tell by now, but I am extremely organized and love making lists. I enjoy having a routine and sticking to it. Life before Ella was very different in the sense that Anna and I had time to do more things. However, after Ella, I had to reset my routine and to-do list expectations because I would be unable to find time to do the things I had planned for the day. I would recommend that you take your to-do list and dedicate half of the list to just taking care of the newborn baby. Some days nothing but taking care of your baby is accomplished, and that is okay because you are entirely responsible for your baby.

It was the first weekend with Ella at home, and I had planned out an ambitious day, which included going to the gym, spending time with Ella and Anna, catching up on a show, and meeting friends at night. In retrospect, I cannot help but laugh at myself. For a single man, this is like a regular and doable day, but for a father with a newborn baby, it is quite an ambitious plan. Good on you if you manage to do this, you are most probably superhuman. I did accomplish going to the gym, but the rest of the day was spent taking care of Ella. I eventually did not get time to watch my show and ended up canceling on my friends. Funnily enough, they knew I was going to bail on them.

It took me a while to resettle into my new routine, which was mostly Anna and I alternating taking care of Ella. However, we also took out time to do what was possible in the window of time we got to ourselves. Remember, self-care is vital for your well-being.

Even stepping out of the house with a newborn can be challenging the first few times. It was daunting for me. Anna had to meet her friends, and I was heading out to do the groceries, so I decided to take Ella with me. Bad idea. Midway, Ella began crying uncontrollably. I had to actually cut my trip short and head home. I fed her with Anna's pumped breast milk and swayed her to sleep. I was aware going grocery shopping was pretty ambitious with a newborn baby, but that is how I learned what not to do the next time I take Ella out alone. After that, I planned my next few outings to be light and easy, such as a walk in the park, sauntering through the aisles at a grocery store, and grabbing a coffee with a friend. These things were easy to escape, and I got to test out how Ella settles in such situations. By doing this, you will get to know your baby better, what time of the day is better suited to them and how much time you can take while you are out. Remember, things like this come with experience, so take it easy.

Your first outing will be nerve-wracking, as was mine, but once you start, it will get easier, and you will become an expert over time. When I took Ella for a walk in the park, it was a whole new experience for me. Walking around with her in the stroller was a different kind of fun. I used to park her stroller near a bench, take her in my lap, and sit with her on the bench, watching people walking by. Birds chirping around us, Ella smiling and moving her cherubic arms around, people smiling and waving at Ella – I do not think I have ever had such peaceful and wholesome moments before in my life. Walks in the park with Ella soon became a form of exercise and a way of bonding with her over her initial years.

A valuable piece of advice I would like to offer to you is to teach your newborn early on to love their crib. It may be easier to have them fall asleep in your arms now, and it may feel heartwarming and perfect, but it will get difficult for you down the road as a parent. It takes some time to get your newborn into this routine, so give it time and be patient. As it is, the first three-month sleep schedule is not easy. The trick is to put your baby down in the crib when they are sleepy and not asleep because you have to train them on how to fall asleep by themselves in their crib. When you or your wife is nursing your baby, make sure they do not fall asleep while nursing. It makes it easier if you think from the perspective of the baby. If you are nursing your baby, he/she falls asleep in your arms, and they wake up in an entirely different place, they will naturally cry – as would adults, if not cry, but be startled. It took Anna and me a while to build a night-time routine for Ella, but we eventually succeeded. Anna would nurse Ella, and then I would read a story and then put her to sleep in her crib. It definitely did not work right off the bat, as there were moments when Ella would start crying when we would try to put her to sleep in her crib, but we were patient, and we managed.

There were moments when Anna would fall asleep, and I would tip-toe over to Ella's crib just to see if she was sleeping sound. There were nights when I would find her wide awake, looking around in amazement with her big deep blue eyes, and then there would be nights when she would be sleeping peacefully. I know it sounds cliché but seeing her in those moments filled my heart with a love I had not felt before. But along with those beautiful and wholesome feelings, there were days when Anna and I would be running on two to three hours of sleep, had not eaten a proper meal, and had not taken a shower longer than two minutes. Those were the days when I felt I was stretched to my limit, and I think I can say the same for Anna. The feeling did not leave me feeling bitter or angry; it was more a feeling of being exhausted and needing a break.

When it comes to sleep, the harsh reality is that you will definitely be sleep-deprived. So, tell yourself sleep is overrated, and for a short amount of time, you will be sleep-deprived. Come to terms with this reality. You and your partner may be waking up every hour to feed the baby or the check on the baby. Since babies grow rapidly, they need constant nourishment.

Here is a fun fact for you: babies sleep 16 hours out of 24 hours in a day but never when we really want them to. By three months, most babies can sleep through the night, and it will feel like heaven when they do that.

Crying is the only way a baby can communicate with you, and when they cry, it usually means they are hungry, tired, need a diaper change, are in pain, or are overstimulated. You will learn how to respond adequately to their cries over time. Expect your newborn baby to cry four hours (minimum) out of 24 hours in a day. This may not be consecutive crying, but it definitely feels like that. They also cry more during evening hours and want to usually eat between 6 pm and 1 am when you are most exhausted. Of course, this can be frustrating, but it is a part of the process. Accordingly, it is important to build your routine around your baby's routine. There will be a lot of reshuffling, a lot of canceled plans, missed appointments, and sleepless nights, but the good news that it is manageable.

Luckily, Anna and I had hired house help, so she managed the daily chores for us. Moreover, we had a strong support system in our family and friends. Anna's mother and my mother were our saving grace. Our friends stepped in to help from time to time whenever we asked them. So, please do not be afraid to ask for help and support whenever you need it, and please believe me when I say you really will need it.

How my relationship with Anna changed after we had Ella

Having a baby changes one's life and will change your relationship as well. You will learn to adjust to new norms, and life will not be the same, which is not necessarily bad.

Anna and I dated for a year, fell in love, then got married. You may have heard that it is easier to fall in love and more difficult to stay in love and keep your relationship nourished and growing. Well, it is true. Your marriage will not work on autopilot mode, and if you leave it at that, you will be setting the ground for an imminent crash.

Anna is the yin to my yang, and we get each other. While we have had our fair share of arguments and fights, we have worked through them in a mature and adult manner. The one thing that really helped us individually and together as a couple was personal therapy. There were epiphanies during my sessions that really changed my outlook on a lot of things. One of the things that resonated with me was self-love.

Did it ever cross your mind that how you feel about yourself could go a long way in deciding the fate of your relationship? Self-love is the biggest contributor to happiness and marriage. How do you practice self-love? It is simple. Trust yourself to make good decisions, allow yourself to feel your emotions, minus the harsh judgment, and treat yourself as valuable (do not confuse that with arrogance).

Self-love is about having a sense of self-sufficiency without tying your happiness and sense of self-worth to someone else. So, go ahead, build and flex your self-love muscle and take good care of your well-being to build a happier narrative of your life.

Anna and I felt we were in a stable position in our marriage and were emotionally, physically, and financially ready to start a family. Having a baby strains relationships in a lot of ways, so please be sure you and your partner are in a good place before you two decide to take such a big step.

One of the biggest issues we dealt with was Anna's postpartum depression. Hormones play a role in how a woman feels after she gives birth to her baby. Oestrogen and progesterone are two hormones that help support a woman's pregnancy, and these levels decline after delivery. Consequently, between five and 14 days after the baby's delivery, women will feel the effect of this. These hormones, combined with stress hormones (which are in abundance since new mothers are pretty stressed about everything from their health to their baby's health), actually cause chemical changes in the brain that affect the mood. There were days when Anna would cry without reason, be irritable, and be on edge, which was completely normal.

At first, I was really overwhelmed and did not know how to pacify her or make it better for her. However, I asked her what she needed from me and what I could do for her. Our communication was centered on our emotional needs a lot during this time. Postpartum blues are extremely common, and around 80% experience these feelings within the first six weeks of delivery. It is very real! It can onset at any point during the first year of the baby's life.

There were times when Anna would stop taking care of herself and would withdraw from friends and family. It was not constant, but it was present. I gave it my best in terms of patience, giving her space, and supporting her. Build a healthy and constructive narrative around postpartum depression with your partner. Fortunately for Anna, she was also seeing her therapist, which helped her during the process.

Male postpartum depression is a big deal, and I went through a depressive phase as well. Fathers aren't immune to depression. Around 7% of fathers suffer from clinical depression within the first three months of a baby's life, and the number reaches 10% higher down the road, between six and 12 months. It was a tough period for Anna and me in dealing with our own emotions, but we gave each other space, time, and patience. It is easy to go to the opposite end and bicker, fight and get even more upset, so it is important to be mindful during this time. You can be each other's best ally or worst enemy through this adjustment phase. If a woman has depression, her partner is more likely to be depressed and vice versa. Hence, be open with your feelings, help each other out and be there for each other.

There are some factors that increase the risk of you having male postpartum depression; lack of sleep, financial stress, relationship stress, history of depression, family history of depression, smoking, and a poor diet. How do you know you have it versus just feeling low? The main difference is that you cannot get out of it and feel stuck. More often than not, you will feel sad or hopeless, have a lot of anger and irritability you cannot get over, you do not care to do activities you used to enjoy, there is a big change in your weight, and you are always feeling tired and lacking energy and if you are having thoughts of death. You are not alone in this, and you can get through it. Following are a few tips that can help you process and work through your male postpartum depression;

- Please get some sleep. You have to make sleep a priority
- Feed your body well. What you put into your body has

an effect on how you feel. Therefore, be sure you are eating healthy.

- Reduce alcohol consumption. It helps you feel better physically and emotionally. Let go of that beer you have been craving and see how you feel after.
- Fill your mind with positive messages and focus on uplifting messages. You will have to do this every day.
- See your therapist and speak to him/her about how you are feeling and how you can work through this period.

Another issue Anna and I experienced was that we had sex less often, our conversations were very to the point, and we would snap at each other more easily (please do not take it personally every time that happens). While women should not have sex for around six weeks after the delivery, it is up to them when they feel ready. When there is so much going on, sex is the last thing on a couple's mind. Sex and intimacy can be difficult for new parents because they will be exhausted, women are going through hormonal changes, and sleep trumps being intimate a lot of times. This did not mean Anna and I loved each other less or were not attracted to each other anymore. It was the reality of the situation. We had to make more of an effort to get into an intimate mood after having Ella.

I did go through some periods where I felt Anna and I had different levels of sexual desire; there were days where I felt rejected, and there were days she felt unwanted, and that is natural. Yet again, because Anna and I have great communication and comprehensive skills, we were able to get our feelings across. Instead of having spontaneous sex, we would now plan when to have sex, which seemed really odd and funny at first, but it really helped us out. When we planned in advance, it also added an element of excitement, as if it was a date.

On our first planned date, both of us actually got dressed and put into looking good for the other, which is another way of conveying how much we care about each other.

Make a mindful effort to spend time with each other. It is a challenge initially; however, you can start off small. Go for a walk together, along with the baby in the stroller, have dinner together when you put your baby to sleep, watch a show together, and order in when the baby is asleep. It starts with the small things. Remember to hold hands, hug and cuddle together.

I consider Anna quite a talkative, as am I, but when Ella was born, our conversations became mere transactions. They mostly went like, "Please hand me her bottle," "I am going to take a shower, stay with Ella," and "Where is the diaper bag?" I remember one particular day when Anna and I literally only spoke in one-word sentences, and when it was time to sleep, I turned to her and said, "How was your day?" and we both burst out laughing. Honestly, it was frustrating at first. It was as if constructing an entire sentence that did not focus on Ella was too much effort for both of us. However, this was something we were aware of and tried to make an effort to adjust. This is where our walks and dinner dates really came in handy. Over the years, this became a habit, we took out time for each other, and it allowed our relationship to remain healthy.

Simply put, yes, your relationship will change, but change is not always bad.

Challenges Millennials face as new parents

Millennials are the generation born from the '80s till the 2000s. So, you can do the math and figure out that there is a huge number of people in the world who are Millennials. Anna and I also fall in this category.

While the generation of baby boomers had their fair share of challenges with child-rearing, Millennials have their different set of issues too. We grew up with technology and screens and witnessed the invention of numerous technologies while growing up. Accessibility and convenience were easier to gain for us as opposed to the generation of baby boomers.

Since technology is so etched within us and is vital in all our lives, it also trickles down to our children. While I was introduced to WhatsApp in my 20s, Ella will most probably know everything about WhatsApp and be more tech-savvy than us by the time she is five. And that is the hard truth. This can go both ways for Ella and us.

The Internet, along with technology, has helped us introduce Ella and keep in touch with relatives who live far away, such as my siblings who live in New York and Brussels. Distance shrinks when we can Zoom call or WhatsApp video call with my brother and sister. I want Ella to be able to recognize them because my siblings are an important part of my life. Hence, in this aspect, technology really works out for me.

Since a baby's brain develops over the first two years of their life, it is imperative that they discover their surroundings and experience the sounds, smells, tastes, and sights. It is vital that you play a lot with your child at this time. However, something Anna and I struggled with as new parents was giving into screen time when we feel exasperated and do not know how to placate her. We are aware that too much screen time is not good for children and their developing minds. Hence, we try to find alternatives and stick to traditional playtime with her. We try to play a lot of imaginary games, take her outdoors, and go for walks with her. However, sometimes when we are really exhausted, we do give her the iPad for a certain amount of time – yes, I feel guilty about this, which is why it happens rarely.

Moreover, if you want to set a healthy precedent for your child in terms of technology and screen time, you have to be very mindful of your relationship with your phone/devices. I am a Twitter geek and keep scrolling for updates every minute, and it is just a reflex action. However, with Ella around, I have reduced my personal screen time and check myself more vigilantly when I am physically around Ella. I am not advocating for you to give up on social media and throw your phone in the furthest corner of your house – just be mindful of your personal screen time around your child. Anna and I have understood that our actions and behavior towards our mobiles and devices will pave the way for Ella's perspective in viewing and using technology when her time comes.

Funnily enough, my parents do not understand this concern because they did not have such issues while raising us.

Another issue that Millennial parents face is financing. Yes, it is generally expensive to have and raise a child, but it is a known fact that Millennials face more of a disadvantage when it comes to having and raising children as opposed to the baby boomer generation. This is due to rising costs and stagnant salaries and wages – essentially, we are doing more with less.

Anna and I both have jobs, and we began saving as much as we could early on in our marriage. However, after having Ella, our daily expenses and costs increased a lot. We have to consider issues such as daycare when both of us return to our jobs. Yet again, daycare was not an issue back in our parents' generation because the mother stayed home, as there was no concept of a career for a woman once a child was born. Nonetheless, trends have changed, and more women are in the workforce than before. Thus, the need for daycares has increased, and because the demand is high, so are costs. Research states that annual average childcare expenses are more costly than housing.

That leaves a lot of Millennial parents in a conundrum.

As the world becomes more competitive, each person's additional or discretionary income has significantly reduced. The situation is even more difficult for Millennials who entered the workforce during the recession and economic recovery. Young adults today are much better prepared than their predecessors in terms of education and skill set. The Millennials today are more likely to have a college degree or postgraduate qualification and additional skill sets than the generation before them, yet they are still trapped in low-paying jobs and struggle financially.

Research and statistics show that, on average, an 18 to 34-year-old makes $2,000 less with each passing year than young workers did in 1980, according to the Census Bureau. Moreover, if these individuals cannot find a way to balance work and raising a family, they are at risk of being trapped within the vicious cycle of low wages.

Due to the nature of Millennials' college degrees, various young workers are beginning to start families while still paying off their student debt. Hence, saving up for their children's college funds could seem like a faraway dream. Due to this reason, numerous Millennials are delaying parenthood until they feel more stable in their financial situation.

Millennials who decide to have children either way often face challenging schedules and struggle with managing their monthly budgets. Young parents are more likely to go to work earlier as well as leave earlier than people without children.

Similarly, young adults with children are twice more likely to work more or work double shifts to meet increasing expenses, and they are also more likely to work late nights to be able to spend time with their children during the day. Despite this, the number of Millennial parents living in poverty is increasing, as per studies and reports.

Thus, it is justified to state that Millennials have their share of stark issues when it comes to raising a family. Therefore, please study your financial situation and career before starting a family. It is always better to plan ahead and weigh the pros and cons.

5

STRIKING A WORK AND HOME LIFE BALANCE

Three months of paternity seemed like a lot before Ella entered our lives. Yet, it whizzed by within the blink of an eye. I do not think any amount of time is enough with a newborn baby. When it was time to return to work, I was a bag of mixed emotions. While I knew I had to resume my 9 to 5 job, I also wished I could stay at home, spend time with and take care of Ella (of course, support Anna as well). Besides, when you are at home for 12 weeks, you get out of the corporate flow. Hence, I was also anxious about the transition back into the corporate life – and more so now because I had a larger responsibility at home – Ella. It was overwhelming, to say the least, but humans are adaptable, so it took me a week to get readjusted into the office routine.

Following are a few tips for you to be able to prepare yourself for returning to work and balancing your priorities;

Prepare yourself mentally before returning to work

A week or two before returning to work, remind your boss or supervisor that you will be returning. Ask a colleague to fill you in on what has been happening in your department in regard to your work, as this will make it easier for you to catch up on everything when you physically return. If you have any meetings to set up, you can do that a couple of days before returning to work. Furthermore, now that you are a father, maybe your working pace will change, so do take that into consideration. Rather than diving back into work headfirst, mentally preparing your mind eases the anxiety and warms you up for what you are getting into.

Speak to your partner about new responsibilities

Since you are returning to work, you will not be around physically to help a lot. Consequently, responsibilities and duties will automatically get reshuffled. It is a good idea to sit with your partner and figure out these new responsibilities and how you two will manage them while you are away at work. Communication and understanding are really great for your relationship because it makes responsibilities and roles clearer. I was unable to be there for Ella during the vast majority of the day, so I opted to wake up earlier, bathe, feed, and play with Ella before going to work so that I could spend time with her and give Anna some extra hours to sleep.

Setting boundaries at work

The reality is that once you become a father, you will not be able to sit around for longer meetings that go into different tangents, such as colleagues speaking about sports or a new show. Moreover, a lot of meetings are also held after official work hours. While I used to be an active part of these conversations and meetings before, I could not anymore after we had Ella because I would rather spend that time at home with my family and cater to their needs. While it may be difficult to set this boundary and assert yourself, you have to take a stand. Building a healthy narrative around timings is something all employees should advocate for, either way. There may be some meetings you cannot miss, and you will stay on for some occasionally, but setting the tone and the boundary makes it easier for your co-workers to know your timings beforehand.

Most corporate cultures do not take such issues into account, and most people will usually hear the following phrases, 'work is work,' 'we had children too and managed just fine not being there.' However, this feeds into an archaic notion and stereotype that men need to be at work regardless, and since the mother is the primary caregiver, what is the need of the father to be there? Just be a bit more mindful of what precedent you set.

Dad guilt

I had heard a lot about mom's guilt but barely heard anything about dad's guilt. Believe me when I say it is a real thing. I missed Ella and Anna, and I felt pretty bad leaving them at home and returning to work. I was fearful that Ella would not be able to recognize me, or she would not want to play with me anymore if I did not see her every hour of the day. At the same time, sometimes work felt more peaceful than home, and I used to feel guilty for feeling that. But hey, we're all human!

Appreciate the co-workers who did your work when you were on leave

Most times, when we are on paternity leave, we tend to forget that our workload is being managed by another colleague of ours. Make sure to thank them and appreciate them for stepping up. Doing so also makes it likely that they will be more understanding and more likely to help out when you have to leave early due to any unforeseen issue at home.

I had quite a few dilemmas initially. There were moments when I was dressed to the tee, about to head out to work, and Ella would poop in her diaper while I was holding to kiss her goodbye. I would think, 'should I stay and change her diaper, or should I hand her over to Anna?' Honestly, I have made easier decisions. Because I have such a supportive wife, she would just reach out her hands and tell me to head to work and that she has it handled. Those were moments of relief filled with pangs of guilt, but I used to tell myself, 'I am doing as much as I can, and I am okay with that.'

There were times when I had a late work meeting, and by the time I would return, Ella would be asleep, Anna would be completely exhausted, and I would feel like a guilty stranger in our own home. But the harsh reality is that it will be like that, and you have to tell yourself you are doing the best you can in your capacity. It may sound like I exist in a utopian world, or maybe I got lucky – but Anna and my workplace were supportive of my entire process, which made me realize how important good support systems can be.

Doing justice to your office work while caring for your child

I enjoy my job and what my field of work offers. It does come equipped with its fair share of challenges, but I do find it to be rewarding. Returning to work after 12 weeks was scary, to say the least. I felt I had forgotten what I had been doing for the past 15 years. There were times at home during my paternity leave when I would get sudden flashes of "what if I forget everything I know by the time I go to work?" Luckily, that did not turn out to be the case.

Since I was working towards setting boundaries in regard to my time, there were also moments when I had to respect the workspace and its rules. It was slightly challenging because I would wonder if I was also overstepping a boundary of theirs. Organizations and corporations have an established set of rules and regulations that we adhere to; thus, while I had my own boundaries to draw in reference to time, they also had their fair share of boundaries, which I respected. That is a given in any professional environment.

Besides, because you have a baby, it is best to be prepared for any unplanned emergencies. Issues such as unanticipated illness or accidents may occur. So, I would advise that once you return to work, have a list of family members and friends who are comfortable with your child, as well as responsible, in case you cannot make it back in time from work or your employer has an issue with you leaving work. This will enable more flexibility and peace of mind for you because you have a backup in case you are unable to leave the office. Various organizations offer emergency childcare perks, so you can check with the HR department beforehand.

One of the most important things, according to me, is communication and honesty. I took my boss into the loop whenever I felt the need. Some would think that they would rather keep their boss out of their domestic issues, but believe me, it really helped when the person who I was answerable to knew my actual situation. Through this, your boss will understand that you respect your workplace and hours as well as recognize that you have urgent issues to tend to at home. When there is more space for empathy, I believe it allows for more flexibility. The last thing an employee would want is for their employer to think they are slacking off. Building a narrative of healthy and honest communication helps debunks such notions from the employers' end.

When I returned to work, I felt I gave it my best with whatever was within my capacity. There will always be so much more that you could have done (pesky thoughts that enter your mind every now and then); however, focus on what you are already doing and be okay with that. Once you give yourself that reaffirmation, everything becomes simpler.

Stop overthinking and feeling dad guilt

We talk about mom guilt quite often, but there is dad guilt as well, which is usually overlooked. It does exist. The feeling of guilt emerges from feelings of shame and not being able to live up to a standard of parental responsibilities.

It usually happens when I am not 100% present or able to partake in the duties Anna is able to do for Ella, such as breastfeeding in the middle of the night and soothing her when she is crying nonstop. However, this guilt is evoked due to society's 'shoulds' of parenting. The truth is that there is no such thing as equal parenting because responsibilities and duties keep shifting. Sometimes, the mother will be doing more, and sometimes, the father will be doing more. Moreover, there are some things that fathers cannot do at all, such as the obvious, which is giving birth to the child and breastfeeding. Hence, know that you are doing enough and be okay with that. You cannot do everything, which is why it is emphasized that the mother and father need to share responsibility.

My guilt even comes up when I have to work long hours at the office or have any sort of social outing, and I feel I am missing out on important moments of Ella growing up. This feeling is hard to quell. I remember Anna calling me on my first day back at work after my paternity leave; she told me Ella was crying a lot because she missed me. At that moment, the pang of guilt and helplessness was a terrible feeling to sit with the entire day.

I was surprised to find that I was not the only one who felt like this. When my group of dad friends and I used to hang out together, they mentioned dad guilt quite often, and I drew comfort from the fact that other fathers felt the way I did. Unfortunately, men are conditioned to be more focused on themselves; hence, switching to a caretaker role once a man becomes a father can lead to unexpected and novel feelings. These feelings usually equate to stress and guilt.

Anna is a certified Pilates instructor and has a studio space where she held classes before we had Ella. Therefore, it was easier for Anna to manage her time schedule and work hours (she is her own boss). When she did resume her Pilate classes, she scheduled classes that were convenient for Ella and her. We summoned the support of our respective mothers and childcare. However, leaving Ella alone, without either of us around, was scary, to say the least. Before Anna resumed work, I had a reassurance that Anna would be home with Ella, but now that Anna was returning to work, I was slightly scared and worried. "Will she be okay?" "What if she gets hurt and none of us are there?" – These questions became a common thought process, and it was tough to break out of it. Initially, it was difficult for Anna and me. We spoke about how we felt and what we could do to lessen our worry. However, we knew our mothers were competent, and we were well connected through the phone. While Anna was busy in class, I was more vigilant with my phone.

Moreover, we started to build our trust with the childcare system. We had heard some scary stories, such as the nanny smoking or drinking in the house, not looking after the child, and nannies sleeping on duty, but we had to have faith in the system. There were more good stories than scary ones, so we had to have confidence that it would work out for the best. Knowing that we have a backup is reassuring. There were times when our mothers could not babysit Ella, and on those days, we would leave Ella with a nanny we hired.

We started researching childcare and interviewing nannies earlier on in order to be better acquainted with them and have Ella get comfortable with the nanny as well. Anna and I, along with Ella, took the nanny we finally chose out for lunch, followed by lunch with just Anna and the nanny. We got a sense of what she was like in and out of her work environment. After that, we decided to have the nanny come in two days of the week, a couple of weeks before Anna resumed her work. Due to this decision, the nanny and Ella got the chance to get familiar with each other. We had cameras installed in the house, so we would also be able to keep a check on everything through our phones whenever we wanted. Having a system in place gives us the peace of mind we need. Luckily, Ella's nanny is wonderful, and she still comes in on days when we need her.

I cannot tell you to stop feeling guilty or overthinking. Nonetheless, I can guide you and tell you that you are doing the best you can. There will always be ups and downs; it is a part of the journey of parenthood. The fact that you are feeling guilty is a testimony to how much you love your child and want to be there for them.

6

THE FUNDAMENTALS OF A NEW BORN BABY'S EMOTIONAL, MENTAL AND SOCIAL DEVELOPMENT (0 - 1 YEAR)

In just a few days after Ella was born, she was so engaged and responsive, constantly following us with her eyes and recognizing our voices. In these early months, parents form trusting bonds with babies by making them feel safe and secure in this world, comforting them, loving them, and meeting their needs.

Even as they grow old (around six months), they are eager to explore, and parents keep it interesting by constantly changing their positions, sometimes on their back and sometimes on their tummy. This lets babies see the world through another perspective, which builds curiosity and helps develop strength, coordination, and physical skills needed later for pushing up, sitting up, and crawling. We began to place toys that Ella could grasp out of her reach when she was six months old, and this let her experience the thrill of moving her body to reach the goal (grasp the toys). By six months, babies can learn how to communicate – not in words but back-and-forth interactions. Parents and caregivers talk and watch to see how babies respond with facial expressions, sounds, and movements. This builds language skills and nurtures social and emotional development in the baby.

By nine months, babies can sit up and freely use both hands to investigate objects, giving them new ways to explore and build their thinking skills. They can also use their fingers to pick up small things, such as bits of food. This, in turn, develops their physical and social-emotional skills as they are able to do more and more for themselves. They even use sounds and actions to communicate, like showing interest in or crawling after a toy they want. When the mother responds by showing how the toy works, it serves as a motivation to keep on communicating. Through this, babies build language, thinking, and social skills.

By 10 months, babies start shaking, banging, filling, and dumping toys. This type of repetition is needed to build thinking skills such as problem-solving and learning how things work. Physical skills also grow during this period. Babies start crawling and start cruising along with furniture and taking their first steps. This is the incredible development that takes place in the first year.

I saw it first-hand in Ella. She went from rolling to sitting to crawling and walking. Babies progress from learning through observation to using their minds and bodies to discover how things work. Babies move from crying as their primary form of communication to expressing a range of needs and emotions through gestures and sounds.

As babies take their first breath, they also need you for the first time. You and your child develop a strong, trusting bond that becomes a blueprint for all future relationships. It provides your child with the courage and confidence to explore the larger world. This loving bond with you is what nurtures your child's successive learning, both now and into the future.

You will notice how much your baby evolves and grows in the first year. There are four categories that the baby grows in; social and emotional, cognitive, speech and language, and motor skill development.

Social and emotional development

A large part of the baby's brain is dedicated to understanding, remembering, and reading faces. A big chunk of our behavior is formed from how we read other people's faces. Make sure you are showing your baby your face and talking to them in a loving and soothing manner. Newborn babies do not understand much of what is happening around them – they can feel but not think. Coming out of the womb physically severs the symbiotic relationship between the mother and the child, but it is developed through caring for and tending to the child again. Their only clue to call out for someone is crying, which usually means they are hungry or tired.

Within the first few months, the baby will start to smile. I remember Ella's first smile, and luckily, Anna and I were around to witness it. It melted my heart. It was the smallest yet most powerful smile I'd seen in my life. Babies even begin to laugh out loud by the time they turn three months old.

Physical development

You will witness a spurt of growth (you know when they say 'they grow up so fast,' – it is true) in the first few months. An important tip to remember is not to jiggle or shake your baby when they cry during the first three months after birth.

That sort of movement can be scary for them. Remember to be gentle with them. Moreover, at this stage, it is easy for babies to be overwhelmed by external stimuli, such as sounds and colors. In terms of hearing, babies had been able to hear while they were in the womb. In reference to sight, because babies have weak eye muscles, they are unable to make sense of visual images. Within the first two months, newborn babies are attracted by bright colors, light, and patterns. Their eyes will begin to move together by the time they turn six weeks. Over the first six months, they will be able to recognize certain faces.

Within the first eight weeks, infants do not have any voluntary control over their bodily movements and are trying to figure out how to make their bodies move. Pulling, sucking, and grasping is reflexes. However, by eight weeks, babies can lift their heads and begin to kick their legs.

Within the third month, babies start to look at their hands and feet, waving them in the air. Thus, physically, they begin to develop a lot during the first year.

Speech and language

For a newborn baby, crying is the only form of communication to get their needs met. Hence, it is vital to respond to and attend to your child's cries during this period so they know that you are there for them when they need you. It provides the child with a sense of security.

Usually, by eight weeks, babies find their voice and begin to make cooing sounds. There is a certain form of communication between you and the baby at this point; you will say something, and the baby will make noises in return. It is suggested that you encourage the development of your baby through the following activities;

- Hang a mobile above their cot
- Speak to them in gentle tones and call them by their name frequently
- Make them listen to music
- Sing to them
- Hold, cuddle and rock them
- Mimic their gestures
- When you talk to them, let them look at your face

Cognitive development

Right from the moment they are born, a baby can see. Newborns' eyes are very sensitive to light; hence dimming light will enable the baby to open their eyes more and look at their surroundings.

They love to look at their parent's faces, patterns, and colors. Newborn babies will focus on faces and objects around eight to 12 inches from their faces. And when a rattle is shaken, they can turn to see where the sound comes from. By the time they turn one year old, they develop a lot cognitively. By now, they are able to drink from a cup themselves, follow directions and identify images correctly.

Signs to look out for in case of a developmental problem

All children are unique and develop in their own time. There are certain benchmarks to adhere to, although all babies will not function accordingly. Be patient with your child during the process of growing and learning. If you are worried about your child's development, seek professional help. There are certain signs to look out for which suggest developmental problems;

- Stiff or limp body (more than usual)
- The baby always has a tight fist
- Not reacting to noise
- Not looking at faces till two months
- Crying for longer than usual periods
- Being extremely quiet
- More than usual difficulties with feeding

It is recommended that you stay vigilant during this period in case any developmental problems arise. If such happens, make sure to get in touch with a doctor. It is better to identify developmental issues earlier on rather than waiting them out.

In order to summarize what to expect from your newborn baby in the first year, refer to the table below;

Birth to three months

- Smiling and following people with their eyes
- Inclined to look at brighter colors
- Gurgle
- Explore their hands and feet
- Able to lift their head while lying on their stomach
- Cry frequently, but feel better when they are held

Four to six months

- Can laugh on top of smiling and are able to imitate sounds they hear
- Can understand that their legs and feet are a part of their body

Are able to sit up

- Can rollover
- Are able to grasp things and begin to put things in their mouth
-

Seven months to a year

- Start to believe they are big and start to take the first steps
- Begin to dance and move to tunes they like
- Play simple games such as peek-a-boo
- Can identify when their name is said out

- Begin to vocalize
- Start to discover, shake, and hit objects together
- Able to look for and find objects hidden out of their sight
- Develop the ability to sit up by themselves
- Build enough strength to pull themselves up to stand and try to walk

Parenting styles and their impact on your child

What exactly is parenting style? It is the standard practice and strategy that parents use in their child-rearing. The idea of parenting styles was introduced in the 1960s by Diana Baumrind, and she draws relationships between parenting styles and basic behavior in children.

You may not know it, but you must be following a certain style of parenting. It is good to be aware of the style you adopt because it does have an impact on your child's outcome and your relationship with your child. More importantly, raise yourself before you raise your child; in simpler terms, this means being more aware of who you are, how you function, and being in tune with your emotions.

There are four types of parenting styles, and they are divided and vary between two dimensions; warmth and control. The first key dimension is warmth; how much affection and love you show to your child.

The second key dimension is control; how much structure you impose upon the child and how involved you are in the child's life, such as setting a bedtime routine, helping with school, and knowing feeding times. Within warmth and control, there are levels of high and low warmth and high and low control, which give birth to the four styles of parenting: authoritative, authoritarian, permissive, and uninvolved. You may find yourself wondering which style of parenting you are practicing, and which style is best for your child's long-term outcome.

I, for one, drifted towards working on being an authoritative parent with Ella, as did Anna. Of course, it is not a constant smooth ride, we would both have our days of switching between parenting styles, and however, we mostly adhered to being authoritative. When we found out Anna was pregnant, we got caught up in the preparations, readying the house, and so on. However, there were many times when I used to sit down with myself and think, 'what kind of parent will I be to Ella?' I used to wonder, 'Will I be strict with her?' 'Will I be a cool dad and allow more candy and screen time?' 'Will I let her do everything my parents never allowed me to?' I did not know till I had Ella. I gravitate more towards authoritative, as I mentioned before, but I am guilty of being permissive a lot of times as well. There are moments when I have been an authoritarian parent with Ella also, but seldom. My go-to style is definitely authoritative, and believes me, I was not born an authoritative parent, and it took me a while to practice it and be mindful of how I am behaving towards Ella. While we are told to be patient and loving with our children, remember to show the same patience and love to yourself as well.

Authoritative parenting (Just right)

The authoritative style is high warmth and high control. Authoritative parents are very loving, affectionate, and offer a sense of structure in the child's life. This type of parent gives reasonable demands and sets consistent limits, and they express warmth and affection and listen to the child's point of view. It is more of a give and takes relationship akin to democracy. Within this style, the parent is still the parent but also expresses warmth. For instance, if the child wants to stay up past their bedtime, instead of saying no, the parents suggest talking about it and ask, 'why do you think you should stay up?' The parent also conveys their concerns to the child, such as 'I do not want you to be tired tomorrow,' and the parent and child come to a compromise.

Such parents usually set rules and encourage the child to follow them for their betterment. Authoritative parents do not use power to gain anything from the child.

Such parents offer guidance in a rationalized manner, which leads to effective communication between the child and the parent. Authoritative parenting is the best style of parenting because it leads to children being emotionally healthy. Children who grow up with authoritative parents are self-assured, great in school, have great social skills, are less involved in alcohol, have good self-esteem, and have better coping strategies.

Authoritarian parenting (Too hard)

Do not confuse authoritarian with authoritative. They are completely different styles of parenting. This is a combination of high control and low warmth. Authoritarianism is more about conformity and obedience and sticks to the orthodox narrative of 'I am the adult, and you are the child.' There is no discussion, and it is a very strict relationship. Such parents are also called helicopter parents. Authoritarian parents wish to shape the behavior and personality of their children according to a certain standard, and if these standards are not met, they are punished.

Usually, there is no logic or rationale behind these set standards the parents wish their children to adhere to. Such parents have high demands from their children, are less engaged, do not encourage open communication, and expect their children to be extremely obedient. If the aforementioned scenario of the child asking for an extension in their bedtime is adapted to this style of parenting, the parent would say 'no' without hesitation, and there would be no room for negotiation.

Children who have authoritarian parents usually turn out to be anxious, withdrawn, and unhappy. They generally have lower self-confidence and poor coping mechanisms. They also lack self-discipline, are associated with poor academic behavior, have unprotected sex, and suffer from substance abuse. Moreover, such children are more dependent on parental guidance since they lack self-confidence.

However, in some cultures, such as Southeast Asian families, such parenting styles are usually equated to authoritative parenting. It is believed that children of these parents turn out to be as mentally healthy as children of authoritative parents.

Permissive parenting (Too soft)

Permissive parenting is characterized by high warmth and low control, the opposite of authoritative. In permissive parenting, children run the show, and anything goes. The parent makes few demands and rarely uses punishment. They try to play the role of a friend rather than a parent. It is not bad to try to be a friend, but there are limits to that. Such parents tend to behave in a very affirmative manner and avoid conflict. Furthermore, permissive parents escape any sort of behavioral control, shirk away from establishing rules, and have fewer expectations from their children. Such parents give the space to their children to partake in activities without thinking about repercussions. This style of parenting has an increased level of responsiveness.

You may have heard the term 'indulgent parent.' It actually means permissive parent. Because such parents demand next to nothing from their children, they are more indulgent, and the children turn out to lack self-discipline. Moreover, the children of permissive parents are generally unhappy and lack the skill of self-regulation. They also do not do well in school and do not respond well to authority.

Uninvolved parents

Uninvolved parents have low warmth and low control. They are, as the title suggests, uninvolved and indifferent to the child's needs, especially emotional needs. They even tend to be neglectful at times. This type of parenting is basically about filling the child's basic needs such as being fed, drinking water, and providing shelter. This is also termed rejecting and neglecting to parent. Such parents usually struggle with substance abuse or are overly involved in careers with no time for their child or family.

There are very low levels of involvement, and these types of parents are generally stricter as well. They do not have demands, neither do they have any responsiveness within them, and they do not show any intimacy towards their child.

Uninvolved parenting leads to emotionally withdrawn, fearful, and anxious individuals. Such children are also more at risk of substance abuse. They have low self-esteem and self-confidence and do not fare well in school.

While parenting styles play an important role in the outcome of a child, it is important to know that other factors are at play in a child's development as well. Factors such as the child's temperament, societal influences, and culture also make up a big chunk of how your child can turn out when they reach adulthood.

The concept of parenting has evolved over the years. Now, parents are much more involved and active in their children's lives. We want to give the best to our children, we want them to be the best, and we want the world to think they are the best. But hey, slow down. The best according to who? Society has millions of standards, and it is not humanly possible to adhere to all of them. Hence, what do you think is best for your child? Give them space and intellectual freedom to explore. Let them develop an innate sense of wonder and give them the freedom to think and discover. Encourage reading, playing, adventure, and outdoor activities. Stimulate their emotional side and encourage them to be in touch with their feelings.

In today's day and age, being worried about every single thing about your child or what your child is doing equates to responsible parenting. Parents generally hover over their children to ensure they are doing everything right because it somehow reflects on them as well. It is important to know that your child is his own person, as are you. Most parents tend to overlook emotions in the chase to be the perfect parent and raise the perfect child. Perfection is subjective hence do the best you can and raise your child to be a kind-hearted and tolerant human because the world needs more people like that. As Frank Pittman once said, "Fathering is not something perfect men do, but something that perfects the man."

7

WORKING ON MY PARENT-CHILD RELATIONSHIP

S o when parents I knew used to say, 'I always put my child before myself,' I would find it hard to believe. There had to be a balance, right? Turns out I was wrong! It is all about the child for the first few months and maybe a year. However, I am not complaining but rather stating the real facts about parenthood. Moreover, it was not just about keeping Ella healthy and functioning; it was also about me building an emotional bond with my child.

Focusing on the needs of my child

Within the first few months, all Ella required was naps, sleep, milk, and diaper changes. While it sounds easy, in reality, it is a non-stop process. Initially, your baby has to be fed every two to three hours, which amounts to eight to 12 times a day. When the child is around three weeks old, you may practice putting off feeding for a short time by engaging in other activities such as rocking or talking to your baby. As the baby grows with each passing day, their nervous system becomes mature enough to handle the slight delay between feeding times. During nighttime feeding, Anna had told me that I should not play or talk to the baby, keep the lights dim and use a soft and gentle voice. By the time they turn two months old, babies automatically eat less at night, and by the time they hit their four-month mark, they begin to get distracted by sights and sounds and delay their feeding time.

I noticed this change in Ella personally. When it used to be my turn to feed her when she was around five months old, it would be more difficult because she was more easily distracted, but during this time, it was also easier to socialize with her during meal times. By the time they hit the six-month mark, most babies begin to eat solid foods. However, before you make the decision to feed your baby solids, consult your doctor.

The next need you will be spending a lot of time catering to will be changing diapers. I was surprised at the number of diapers Anna and I would change in a day. You do not have a choice because you cannot let urine or poop sit in the diaper for too long – it causes skin irritation. You may have to change at least three to six in a day.

And then comes another important need; sleep. To be honest, I loved and needed to sleep a lot at this age as well. When Ella was a newborn, she used to sleep for around 17 to 18 hours a day, but not on a go. She usually used to wake up after every two to three hours. They need to wake up because they have to be fed. It will remain like this for the first few weeks. There are a few things to note in a baby's sleep cycle. There are murmuring periods for around every hour while the baby sleeps, and this is known as active sleep. Besides that, the sleep cycle consists of drowsy sleep, deep sleep, and active sleep. During drowsy sleep, babies can be awakened easily. During deep sleep, they are not awakened easily, and during active sleep, the baby is restless and has rapid breathing.

During the first couple of months, I noticed that Ella would sleep through loud noises as compared to when she was around four months old. It is important to establish a bedtime routine for your baby because, during this age period, they sleep for at least seven to eight hours. I used to sing and rock Ella to sleep in a dim room, which would help her fall asleep faster. As Ella grew up, it would be more difficult to put her to sleep because of all the adrenaline and excitement they feel throughout the day. Hence, I strongly suggest you set a routine when they are three months old and build it up.

Another need of a newborn baby is naps. Naps become common as they grow older. When I used to run errands with Ella, it would be tempting to make her nap so I could go about doing my thing easily. As lovely as it sounds, it is not practical because you do not want your child to be constantly napping, as it destabilizes their set schedule. When your baby turns six months old, make them take longer naps during the day and increase the time between each nap time – it leads to better sleep at night. Make sure you establish a set routine for nap times and adhere to it as much as possible.

The importance of building an emotional tie with your child

As I mentioned earlier, it is necessary to be there to fulfill the needs of your child, but it is also important to focus on building an emotional bond with them. Since I had taken paternity leave, I think I was able to bond with Ella quite a bit during the first three months.

A baby's brain has a lot of growing to do, and you can help it develop through bonding with them – lots of smiles, cuddles, and loving words. For some fathers, bonding happens right away, and for others, it may take some time. Know it is never too late to bond with your child. Physical affections make babies grow. Try cuddling your baby close to the left side of your chest so they can hear your heartbeat. Your baby may find it reassuring. Besides, skin-on-skin contact, such as a baby massage, can make your baby also feel secure.

Eye contact is especially good for bonding development. When your baby deliberately catches your eyes, you can look right back into their eyes and maintain eye contact till they look away. Furthermore, babies love to hear you talk, so give a running commentary as you go through the day, talk about what you are doing and name the things and objects around you. Babies also love sing-song voices and funny noises. Using facial expressions when you talk helps your baby learn the connection between words and feelings. When your baby starts to babble, you can repeat the sounds they make and practice taking turns at making conversation. During the time I used to spend with Ella, I would be speaking to her as if she were an adult. I would tell her about my day, my work, and my general feelings. In return, she would smile and make babbling noises. It is one of the most adorable communications. I actually used to look forward to coming home from work and just holding her in my arms and speaking to her. It was my time with her, and it helped build a bond between us.

It is never too early to start reading to your baby. Babies love looking at the pictures in books, listening to your voice, and spending time with you. Singing songs is a fun way to develop your baby's language skills. Try it in the car, in the bath, at bedtime, even if you are off-key. Your baby will love the rhythm and will be soothed by your voice. I do not have the loveliest of voices, but I found a rapt audience in Ella. She was one person who would love smiling, bobbing up and down, and gurgling whenever I would sing to her.

Smile at your baby. When they see you smile, they release chemicals in their body that help them grow and make them feel good. And who does not love a baby smiling? It is the most pleasing feeling.

Play simple games with them, such as peek-a-boo and pat a cake. This can help with their learning and movement skills. If you find that your baby's gaze is averted, that means they may not want to play anymore or might begin to get tired. If that is the case, try a change of activity, put them on the floor to gaze around, or put them to bed for a nap.

It does not take much for a father to bond with his baby. It is the small things you can do; they go a long way. Other than the fact that it is a beautiful connection, there are also benefits to fathers bonding emotionally with their children. Due to fathers spending time with their child, the child's mental and physical development is enhanced as opposed to children whose fathers do not take an active role in their upbringing. Moreover, fathers feel less stressed and more confident when they build a bond with their children. I can vouch for that. Spending time with Ella, be it speaking to her, holding her, or playing with her, always made me feel less anxious or stressed, especially if I had a long and grueling day. Furthermore, research highlights that solid father and child bonds deter future issues like depression, crime, and drug abuse. Such children also fare better at school and have successful relationships with loved ones. What's more, is that grown male adults who had a healthy relationship with their fathers during their childhood were better able to handle stress and anxiety.

Hence, it is imperative that fathers spend valuable time with their children and help them become healthy, functioning adults. Most fathers are guilty of getting caught up in their jobs and building their careers. After all, their justification is that they are doing it for their children. However, it is equally important that you provide for them emotionally as well, not just financially. They also justify not being wholly present by thinking the mother is already with the child, and that should be enough, but I am sorry to say that it is not enough. You share an individual and special relationship with your child, as does your partner.

Over the years, your relationship with your child will evolve differently in comparison to your partner's relationship with your child. You cannot expect the mother's presence to be enough, nor can the mother expect the father's presence to be enough in the child's life. Taking out time in the day for your child and family needs to be a priority and one that should not be overlooked.

Understanding the type of attachment you have with your child

The types of attachment styles were first categorized by Mary Ainsworth in the '70s, and her work was inspired by John Bowlby's (the inventor of attachment theory) work, which came about in the '50s. Attachments are a continuous process of pursuing and upholding a level of proximity with another individual. Expectations that people have from relationships with others, built on the relationship with their primary caregiver as infants, are known as attachment styles.

Attachment styles play an essential role in the healthiness of our relationships, relationships with partners, the workplace, and with friends. The attachment theory argues that a strong emotional and physical bond to one primary caregiver in our first years of life is critical to our development – it sets the template for building relationships with people. Over time, we use this same template in all our relationships. If our bonding is strong and we are securely attached, then we feel safe to explore the world. We know there is always that safe base to which we can return at any time. However, if our bond is weak, we feel insecurely attached. We are scared to leave or explore a rather scary-looking world because we are afraid that we cannot return. After having read about attachment styles, I automatically began to think about my attachment style with my mother and father. Furthermore, it also made me more mindful of the type of attachment style I want Ella to create with me. Sometimes, we do not realize how much attachment styles influence us.

There are four types of attachment styles that your child can develop with you. They are as follows;

- **Secure** (Flexible, treat each relationship as it is, effective at problem-solving)
- **Anxious – Ambivalent** (Clingy, a lot of unaddressed needs)
- **Anxious – Avoidant** (Much more independent, tell themselves they do not need a relationship, tend to escape situations where people want to express strong emotions because it makes them anxious)
- **Fearful** – Avoidant (Combination of the above two; conscious need to have a deep relationship, but very afraid of abandonment and their behaviors are erratic)

Knowing about attachment styles beforehand enables you to be more mindful of the attachment style you want to establish between yourself and your child. Most times, when people are unaware of their own attachment style, they will parent their child in the same way they were parented by their parents.

Secure

Children who have a secure attachment with their primary caregiver get distressed when their caregivers are not around and become happy when they are around. When secure children are scared, they turn to their parents to seek comfort. Any contact – physical or emotional – is accepted wholly by securely attached children. Moreover, such children prefer parents over strangers.

How do parents of securely attached children behave? Well, they take out more time to play with their children, are quick at responding to their needs, and are more responsive to their children in comparison to the other attachment styles. Additionally, there are five primary conditions needed to cultivate a secure attachment style with your child.

- **Felt safety:** The child must feel safe, and this establishes trust. Safety and protection do not just mean locking in a car seat, or the crib is secure. Rather, it means soothing a child after they hear a loud noise and get frightened. This helps the child internalize that someone is there for them and can help them – hence the world is safe for them.

As a parent, you may think you have a tall order of immediate needs to respond to at all times; however, the motto to follow here is 'more often than not.'

• **Feeling seen and known:** The apparent behavior is atonement to understand the inner state of what your child's internal world is like. This is important because the child has one cry, and it is up to the parent to decipher whether it is a hungry cry, pain cry, or asleep cry. It is a personal intuition when you feel your child is behaving in an offhanded manner. This, in turn, helps the child with their self-development because they know they have something, and someone is out there trying to help them figure out what it is.

• **Felt comfort:** The child needs to internalize these feelings. It is not just about picking the child up when they cry while looking at your phone; it is also important to be mindful and present with your child while soothing them so they receive the internal message that when they are upset, they will be comforted, it is not the end of the world, and their need is being met – remember to tell yourself 'More often than not.' They will be taught through parental behaviors how to have emotional regulation, which they will be able to do themselves as they grow up. Through this, they will learn to internalize self-soothing.

- **Feeling valued:** The only way to create self-esteem in a child is that the child has a sense of accomplishment and that the parent or caregiver rejoices in that sense of accomplishment. This is called amplifying the effect. The child then feels really good about themselves, which is how self-esteem is created. Since children learn through their eyes and not their ears, what you can do is show appreciation and acknowledgment through body language, expressions, and verbally. Since most of this is felt before actual words develop, words do not mean as much as a loving look or an adoring look. They assess everything in the world through how you present it to them.

- **Felt support:** This feeling comes a bit after infancy. When the child is encouraged to be who they are and are motivated to explore their own interests while they have your support, they feel they can go off in the world and find their own path because they believe there are people in the world who want the best for them.

You know you have a secure attachment style with your parent or child if you have confidence in your partner and relationship. Feelings such as trust, comfort, connection, space to grow, healthy independence from each other, and communicating loving feelings are common in such an attachment. Such individuals are able to provide support to their partners and reach out for help when they need it. Furthermore, securely attached children tend to become more empathic and mature adults in the future.

In a study, researchers discovered that women with a secure attachment style harbored increased positive feelings with their romantic adult relationships as opposed to women with an insecure attachment style.

Anxious – Ambivalent

Children who form the anxious ambivalent attachment style have parents who were inconsistent with their caregiving and meeting the child's emotional needs in a stable and consistent manner. Most times, parents may act like this on an unconscious level. For instance, if a parent hears their child crying for warmth or affection, the parent fulfills their need sometimes and sometimes doesn't and lets the child resort to self-soothing. Hence, the caregiver comes off as unpredictable to the child. This gives rise to the feeling of internal conflict within the child – they are happy when the parent is attentive and confused and sad when the parents are not attentive, hence the term ambivalent attachment.

On the one hand, they doubt the caregiver, and on the other, they also yearn for the caregiver's attention to meet their emotional needs, so they end up clinging to them. This lays the foundation for the child's ambivalent behavior pattern, and it usually pans out as indecisiveness and uncertainty.

As an adult, this usually comes out in a lot of indecision in making even the simplest of decisions. What to eat, what to wear, where to go on holiday. Moreover, deciding becomes more difficult when an individual feels conflicted, hence the feeling of ambivalence. Moreover, they become clingy romantic partners and feel insecure about exploring the world around them.

In an experiment conducted by Ainsworth, she observed how after time apart from their mothers, a few children were confused, restless, and evaded eye contact with their mothers upon reuniting with them. However, at the same time, the children were observed to be extremely clingy with their mothers upon reuniting with them. While the child was channeling all its energy towards staying next to and around the mother, it seemed that the child was unable to derive any comfort from her presence.

While the parent or caregiver is away from an anxious ambivalent child, they will become visibly upset and angry. However, while they resist being soothed upon being reunited with the parent, they cling to the parent regardless because they are seeking safety from them. Anxious ambivalent babies have very high emotional needs and feel they cannot go on without support from others, and yet they are ambivalent because when they turn to others for help, they are turned down or hurt in return. Thus, they are stuck in a loop. Some of these babies are very difficult to soothe.

Being an anxious ambivalent child can affect how the child socializes and the way they comprehend and perform tasks. Since they are so caught up in trying to attain the attention of their parents or caregiver, they are unable to absorb any information or instructions. Most times, in a school setting, the 'class clown' stereotype is an anxious ambivalent child. Such behaviors in a school setting can often lead to a misdiagnosis of attention deficit hyperactivity disorder (ADHD) when in actuality, they feel extreme anxiety in their internal world. The sense of self in an anxious ambivalent child is very shaky because, deep down, they feel unlovable and unwanted. Nonetheless, at the same time, sometimes people have been there for them, so maybe they are lovable? There is a lot of confusion. And maybe the best way to characterize the sense of self within such children is what other people think of them.

In a school setting, there can be a mixed presentation of how severe attachment issues are and whether or not relationships have been hurtful in the past. On the lighter side, you can see a child who likes to be the center of attention and is preoccupied with what people think instead of focusing on their school work. On the desperate side, such children tend to get into intense and bad relationships, get mad when relationships fail, and look for signs of abandonment and failure even when there aren't any. They never feel satisfied in relationships. They always know something is wrong and feel there is something to be worried about, which is not a healthy mind space to be in.

Anxious avoidant

This type of attachment style usually develops within the first 18 months of a child's life. Usually, parents of an anxious-avoidant child are not present and around so much in their life and ignore the child's needs by responding in a manner that is rejecting the child. Moreover, any emotions and feelings shown by such children are usually frowned upon or dismissed by the parent or caregiver because the parent may want to avoid emotions as well.

This style of parenting pushes children towards forming a premature sense of independence. Since such children's needs are not being met – intentionally or unintentionally – as they grow older, they begin to look after their own needs, self-soothe and create a false sense of independence. Due to this, they feel they do not need anyone to support them and can take care of themselves.

An anxious-avoidant parent or caregiver may move away physically from their child when the child shows fear or sadness and shame their child for showing emotion and feelings. Moreover, such parents and caregivers want their children to become independent, which may not be possible for their age. Phrases such as 'grow up,' 'do not cry,' or 'you are behaving like a baby' are used when their children show any signs of emotion. Hence, the child feels it is pointless to cry out for attention from the caregiver or parent and suppress their internal need and desire for love and showing any sort of emotion because it will end up getting rejected and put aside. Because emotions are shunned by the caregiver or parent, the child stops showing them. Through this suppression, they can still be close to the caregiver or parent. Growing up in such an emotionless environment can lead to a strong sense of rejection within the child, and their attachment system shuts down, therefore creating a vast disconnect from their needs.

In the aforementioned experiment conducted by Ainsworth, anxious-avoidant children evaded contact with their mother once reunited with them. Even though they put up an external façade of not needing their mother, they acted just as anxious and distraught as securely attached children when separated from the mother, except they made an effort not to show it. Avoidant children want to stay close to their caregiver but without actually having to interact with them.

Children who develop an anxious-avoidant style of attachment are usually precocious, seem very self-contained, and seldom show signs of needing any sort of love or warmth. Over time, they eventually forget they have feelings and have very little awareness of emotions. Does that not sound unhealthy? However, they do have good self-regulatory abilities. They like to take care of themselves and enjoy exploring the world because it distracts them from relationship anxieties.

While such children may like to socialize, they might have a problem connecting with people and feel they should not depend on others for anything. They may look calm, but deep down, they feel a lot of anxiety.

As adults, they become external-focused and accomplishment and achievement-focused. In relationships, they usually shirk away from emotions and intense situations and withdraw because they feel overwhelmed and disconnected from the situation.

Fearful Avoidant

This style of attachment is also known as disorganized. This is the worst type of attachment style a child can form. Children who suffer from abuse and trauma usually form this attachment style. Such children's parents or caregivers behave chaotically, and the children see them as scary because of their aggressive behavior. They do not feel safe in this world either.

Usually, such parents exhibit unpredictable and erratic behaviors in their parenting methods. They may be extremely loving on some days and may not meet the child's basic needs on other days, which in turn gives birth to a sense of fear in the child for their safety.

Being exposed to trauma and emotional abuse has the ability to cause long-term harmful effects on the child, which alters the emotional regulation of the child's brain. Unconsciously, the child figures out that the caregiver or parent cannot meet their needs. Then again, the parent's behavior may not always be intentional. Such parents may have also had a disordered type of childhood. Since most parents parent in the same way they were parented, their actions may be unintentional. Parents of fearfully avoidant children have not worked through their own trauma, hence allowing the trauma to internalize and affect their behavior over time. They can get easily triggered by a child's cry and dissociate from their child.

Caregivers or parents of fearful-avoidant children may have low confidence in raising a child. Hence, they get scared and are overwhelmed by the entire process. Due to this, the child seems terrifying to them, which prompts the caregiver to behave unpredictably. While they might reward a certain behavior of the child, they may also punish the child for the same behavior on another day. This will obviously leave the child scared and confused. The most important person in the child's life – the primary caregiver – from whom they desire warmth, love, and connection becomes a source of fear for them.

Consequently, due to the unpredictability of the caregiver's actions, fearful-avoidant children cannot figure out how to have their needs met and are left clutching on to nothing, feeling confused. Imagine being a child and experiencing such feelings. It is alarming, to say the least.

In the aforementioned study by Ainsworth, fearful-avoidant children were observed to behave in a conflicting manner towards their mothers. They were noted as running towards the caregiver but then changing course midway and running away. They would also act out against their mother. Since the child yearns for comfort from the mother, they automatically want to be near them and with them, but in a fearful-avoidant child, being near the mother also triggers a sense of warning and fear.

Such children usually stare at their caregiver or parent but tend to avoid eye contact, shout and wail non-stop to grab the caregiver's attention, and display conflicting emotions, such as needing attention and then shirking away from it right after getting it.

Older fearful-avoidant children find it difficult to self-soothe and find it hard to open up to other people. Due to them feeling unsafe and not secure in the world, they seem to be searching for the next negative occasion. Moreover, such children do not know much about personal boundaries and tend to talk about inappropriate issues with strangers. They seem to act the same way towards people they know and strangers, have no sense of guilt and have difficulty concentrating and maintaining friendships and romantic relationships in their adult life. As adults, they may dissociate, just as their caregiver did, have low self-esteem, have trust issues, seek constant approval, and tend to gravitate towards abusive relationships.

Such children will need therapy since the behaviors they resort to can be damaging.

A newfound connection with my father

I do think it is justified to say that my relationship with my father was extremely strained or broken. I thought I had a completely normal relationship with my father up until I began therapy and became a father myself. My father never hurt me intentionally; it was just unfortunate that he was not around as much when we were growing up.

I was around nine years old, and I had received an award at school. I remember holding the award extremely carefully all the way home from school. My mom hugged and congratulated me and even gave me a Popsicle as a reward. When my father came home, I ran to him excitedly to show him the award as well. However, all he did was smile, pat me on my head, and return to whatever he was doing. I think my mom noticed the look of dejection on my face.

As I had mentioned earlier, my mother was our primary caregiver, and because parenting was way different in their generation, my father not helping out and being around was not a big deal. He would be with us on weekends, watch TV with us, and read to us. I know he wanted me to be an engineer or a doctor, careers which I did not aspire towards. Growing up, he would sit me down and talk to me about medicine, how trains worked and how planes flew. Now that I look back, I think that was his way of showing his interest in my life. When I opted to take accounting as a major, he was upset with me, but luckily, he could see I enjoyed it and supported me. He is a man of few words, has a very strong sense of wrong and right, and does not express himself too much. Therefore, I never confided much in him. Even as adults, our conversations mostly centered on sports, the weather, and politics – the clichés. Beyond that, I found it difficult to have a conversation with my father. It did not make me love him less, but I feel I never really connected with him how I would have liked to.

I know I did not want to be that type of father to Ella, so I feel I behave in the opposite manner. I am emotionally and physically present for Ella, play with her, support her, help her explore, tell her how much I love her, and appreciate her for the smallest of things. Maybe this is me making up for what I did not receive as a child from my father – filling in the gaping wound my father left me with – a wound that called out for love and attention.

However, becoming a father, something shifted within me. I somehow discovered a newfound love for my father as well. Yes, I was aware that my father had wounded me as a child – abandonment and neglect wounds, to be more specific – nevertheless, I worked through it with my therapist and came to the point where I was able to forgive him for doing that. Moreover, I took out time to speak to him (after we had Ella) and tell him how much I had expected from him as a child and how he was unable to meet those expectations of mine. It was a sad conversation, to say the least. I felt I had hurt him by telling him how I felt, and seeing him sitting across me, slightly hunched with greying hair, broke my heart, but I needed to tell him.

In turn, he told me that he tried to be the best father he could be, and he was sorry for not being able to do more for me. Having heard that from him somehow made me feel lighter – it was an apology I did not know I was looking for. Moreover, it made me realize he was human and made mistakes, and I allowed myself to look at things from his perspective. Having this conversation worked in favor of our relationship.

See, you do not just become a father by giving birth to a child. It takes effort to build a relationship. I find myself being able to talk more easily to my father now, and sometimes we go for a walk with Ella, and we have found a new hobby – Tamiya plastic model kits. He has started to keep more in touch via texting and calling, and I cannot begin to tell you how much I appreciate that. I suppose it is his way of trying to make up for lost time with me. And it is not just me. He is working on becoming more vocal with my other siblings, as well as my mom. It is heart-warming, to say the least. What's more, is that his relationship with Ella has benefited a lot, and he is more loving and affectionate towards her than he was with us. Being a father is not easy. Hence, when I became one, it made me empathize with my father, which helped us improve our relationship.

8

_____

EFFECTIVE PARENTING

After Mirabelle gave birth to Ella, time had no meaning for us. Yes, we were a family now, and Ella was the most beautiful addition to our lives but taking out time for ourselves became increasingly difficult. Regaining a sense of self after having a child is hard to do because you are lost in your day-to-day care. Take out time to find yourself again. I was a bag of emotions in the first few months. You may be feeling a myriad of emotions; happiness, sadness, gratitude, or surprise – whatever emotions you are feeling, allow yourself to feel them because it is okay.

Self-care and managing my emotions

While you may find yourself sitting and staring into space, at the back of your head, you will be aware of your baby's whereabouts, what they are up to, and if they are safe or not – that can be mentally tiring as well. You will always find yourself occupied or preoccupied. Being busy and always being on your toes is somehow seen as a positive aspect nowadays. Well, it is not.

Take a deep breath and step back. If you and your partner burn out, you will not be able to be there for your child. Simply put, it is mentally and physically exhausting and draining. Your emotions are all over the place, and you are juggling between your family, your newborn baby, your job, and the house. Where do you fit in? Being the best father to our child and practicing effective parenting requires us to be the best version of ourselves, and in order to do that, we need to make intentional choices and changes in our life to look after ourselves. Fortunately, as Millennial parents, the idea of self-care is extremely important.

Following are some tips for being an effective parent and taking care of your needs;

- Dedicate time to yourself: Make self-care a priority. Even taking a few minutes for yourself on a daily basis will help you face the day with a clearer mind.
- Turn self-care into a habit: It needs to be something that everyone in the family knows is happening for you. Once your family knows your boundaries, they will respect them, and it becomes normalized.

- Establish some realistic expectations from yourself: The best way to do this is to think about optional versus necessary. For instance, your daily share in the household chores can be optional but keeping the house safe for your child is necessary.

- Make to-do lists: It becomes easier to see what you have to do as opposed to what you need to do. Plus, it makes it easier to keep a tab on all your commitments in the day.

- Ask for help: Mirabelle and I hired house help, which was a blessing. We had our family and friends, and that really allowed us time for ourselves. If you have the option, reach out for help or hire help if your finances allow you to.

- Take out much-needed me-time: What do you define as me-time? Is it going to the gym, going for a walk, sipping on coffee and doing nothing, watching your favorite show, scrolling through your Twitter or Instagram feed, or reading? Whatever it may be, make sure to carve out that space for yourself because it helps you feel re-energized and more fulfilled.

- Make plans with other people: You are much less likely to give up on an appointment if someone else is involved. It could even be a 30-minute coffee plan or a jog in the park with a friend.

- Keep a journal: If you feel overwhelmed with emotions, try keeping a journal and writing down what you are feeling. Penning your thoughts down relieves stress and allows for introspection.

- Exercise: Make sure you get in some form of physical exercise every day, even if it is for 20 minutes. Exercising improves your mood as well as your mental health.
- Take a break from electronics: In the 21st century, not being glued to your phone is akin to blasphemy. However, always being on your phone is not healthy. Sometimes, it is good to disconnect from electronic devices.

Remember, taking out time for yourself does not make you a bad father! Believe me when I say it works wonders when you make time for yourself. Start off small and build a routine if that helps. Mirabelle and I spoke about our own self-care and self-time, and we knew when the other had their personal time and would respect that. Moreover, I always felt more re-energized and in a better mood after I took time to do my own thing, which was going to the gym and watching a show on Netflix. When Mirabelle would go for a spa day or a walk in the park, I would look after Ella and vice versa. I believe it helped Mirabelle and I maintain a healthy relationship with ourselves as well as with Ella.

9

ADVICE FOR NEW DADS

B eing a dad is not easy, and that little bundle of joy can bring new dynamics to your relationship. Following are a few concerns most new fathers have, and I will tell you how to work through them.

How to keep your relationship healthy

- Listen to your partner: Instead of trying to solve your partner's problems, just hear her out. Men have a tendency to go into a problem-solving mode instead of listening at times. Ask her what she needs from you and be more empathic.
- Do not complain a lot: Your partner carried the baby and gave birth, so while you may be dealing with mood swings

and being low, it is nothing compared to what she had to go through. Hence, be mindful of complaining to her.

- Offer help unsolicited: Do not ask if she needs help. Instead, make a statement to help. If she usually cooks, tell her, "Hey, I will make dinner tomorrow," instead of "Do you want me to make dinner tomorrow?"
- Plan time away from the child: If you can do a weekend, an overnight stay, or even dinner for a couple of hours, do it.
- Give her compliments: Something non-physical or non-sexual, preferably. Tell her what a great mom she is or how you appreciate her.
- Say I love you more: Send a text or leave a note whenever you can but do not make it sexual. Just be loving and nice.

Do not take things personally

Your baby is not out to get you, it may feel like that sometimes, but your baby is just making sense of the world around them. Your baby will cry and whine, and this may stress you out initially. If your baby cries when you hold them, just hold them more often. If they cry when you bathe them, do it more often. Babies thrive on familiarity, so things being done repeatedly create comfort between you and them.

Focus on quality of time, not quantity of time

If you have a lot of time available or are the primary caretaker, that is great. However, for many new dads, we may feel guilty for not spending enough time with our babies. We feel the more time we spend, the better it is. But spending a lot of time also conflicts with our work schedule or other commitments. What is quality time? It is being present at the moment, giving affection, playing, or feeding – it is being specifically focused on your child and not distracted by your phone or having a conversation with someone else. Spend one-on-one time with the baby as well. There is something special when you spend time alone with your baby. It becomes fun, and you become confident in your ability as a dad. It allows you to connect, talk and play with your child.

Be okay with your mistakes

We all make mistakes as first-time fathers, so accept them, learn from them, and move on. It does not mean that you are not capable of taking care of your child; it just means you lack experience. You may not have changed the diaper properly or miscalculated their nap time, and that is okay.

Enjoy the present

When you are a new dad, you will often think about the future. 'I cannot wait till she walks or talks.' You do not want such thoughts to overshadow the current stage your child is in, so just enjoy that stage for the time being. You will not get that time back because time goes by fast. Before you know it, your child has grown. Hence, the time to do it is now. Being a dad is not about trying to handle every 'what if' that could come along as much as it is about being in the moment.

Be confident in yourself

We get overwhelmed, nervous, and stressed, and that is okay, but you have to have confidence that you will be able to do this. It might feel like a lot, so do not feel sorry for yourself. Focus on what you can do and not what you cannot do.

Adaptation

Time management becomes difficult, and you will have less personal time. You will have to figure out what you really want to do and then coordinate with your partner. Having a child will add more responsibilities. Whether it is time, cleaning, or finances, you will feel like you barely have time and no control over it. A lot of decisions will be made around the baby's schedule, and you will have to get used to it.

To be honest, I tried to do as much reading and learning as I could before Ella was born, but the real lessons began when I first held her in my arms. It is an ongoing process, and you learn on the job. So, enjoy the small moments, laugh at the mistakes, take it as it comes, and you will be okay!

EMBRACING THE CHANGE AND THE JOURNEY

Congratulations! You are becoming a father or are already a father to a beautiful child. Your journey with your child will be as special as you choose to make it. You are starting a new chapter in your life.

Before I had Ella, I could count the number of times I had held a baby, so the change was daunting. However, Mirabelle and I have turned out to be great parents, thanks to the honest communication, support, and love we offer each other. The day I found out Mirabelle was pregnant with Ella, I did everything I possibly could to prepare myself and our home for Ella. I was there for my wife and daughter whenever I had the chance, and in retrospect, I am extremely happy with my decisions.

Of course, we had a fair share of ups and downs, as there were days when I thought I would pull my hair out, and there were days when I did not want anything other than my family around me. Is life very different when you become a father? Nearly all men will be concerned that having a child will impact their life. Having a child does not change who you are but can impact different areas of your life. Some men will view that change as positive, while others may view it in a negative light, and the good news is that you get to decide. You are up in the middle of the night because your baby is crying. You could either curse the world and be extremely annoyed or look at your child's face and tell yourself how lucky you are. You get to decide how you will approach the situation.

Your journey will be more or less the same, you will be stepping into a new realm, and I want to tell you that you will succeed.

Following is a checklist I have prepared for you to tackle all the changes you will be encountering and to prepare you for the pregnancy. You can refer to it anytime you find yourself feeling lost and in need of guidance. Tick off the things you have completed in order to feel you have accomplished something amidst the change you are witnessing. This list can help you prepare everything before your newborn baby arrives in this world;

- Feel and practice gratitude
- Take responsibility for your own emotions
- Get involved with your partner
- Buy minimum necessities for the child
- Improve your financial situation

- Start saving (if you haven't already)
- Read, watch videos, attend birthing classes
- Prepare a nursery for your child
- Baby proof the house
- Ask for paternity leave
- Communicate honestly and effectively with your partner
- Build a support system with family and friends
- Find a suitable health plan and birth for the pregnancy
- Help your partner prepare her hospital bag and the
baby's hospital bag
- Prepare your own bag
- Take out time for yourself

Good luck on your new journey. I hope you find it in yourself to know that you are already doing a wonderful job at trying to be the best dad you can be – you reading this book is a sign you care.

Thank you for taking out time to read this book. I hope it helped you out. Kindly put a review on Amazon.

If you thought it was helpful in any way, I would appreciate it if you could leave a review on Amazon, along with any feedback and suggestions you would have liked to see in the book or other books in the future.

You can mail your feedback and suggestions to books@alfiethomas.com.

ACKNOWLEDGMENTS

I would not have been able to write this book without the help of my supportive and loving wife, Mirabelle, and my beautiful daughter, Ella, who has taught me so many new things in life. At the center of this book, there are numerous people amongst my family and friends who have helped me along the journey of penning down what it is to be a father, sharing their feedback, being patient with me and always taking an interest in my passion to write. I thank you all for being there with me every step of the way. I would not have been able to do it without your support, motivation, and love.

QUICK NOTE

Positive reviews from awesome customers like you help others to feel confident about choosing this book too. Could you take 60 seconds on Amazon or any platform where you got the book and share your happy experiences? There are other awesome books like *The First Time Father, The First Time Father: Baby's First Year, Sleep Training like a Pro, Single Dad Parenting like a Pro, Potty Training Like a Pro, Discipline Like a Pro, All Fathers Memorable Jokes* and others still to come. Any ideas you would like Alfie Thomas to write about or improve on, his email is always open. You can reach out to books@alfie-thomas.com and https://thealfiethomas.com/

https://mirabellen.activehosted.com/f/1,
https://www.facebook.com/groups/1253933881690907, and https://www.instagram.com/alfiethomas.official/

We will be forever grateful. Thank you in advance for helping us out.

Printed in Great Britain
by Amazon